FINDING OUT ABOUT

Modern
Farming

Contents

This edition published 1990 by
Franklin Watts
96 Leonard Street
London EC2A 4RH

ISBN 0 7496 0347 X

Original edition published 1987 by
Hobsons Publishing plc
Produced in conjunction with and sponsored by
The Association of Agriculture, the British
Agrochemicals Association, the Fertiliser
Manufacturer's Association, the NFU and the
Wates Foundation

Acknowledgements

We would like to thank the following for supplying photographic material:

Andy Burridge
Birds Eye, Walls
British Wool Marketing Board
Cowper & Co Perth
Farming Information Centre
Food from Britain
Ciba Geigy
Hardi Ltd
The Hereford Herd Book Society
Institute of Agricultural History and Museum of
English Rural Life, University of Reading
Landsaver
Lingarden Limited
Massey Ferguson
Meat & Livestock Commission
National Dairy Council
Norsk Hydro Fertilizers
Philip Steele/ICCE
OXFAM
Pig International
Plant Breeding Institute
Poultry World
The Royal Veterinary College
The Apple and Pear Development Council
Farmers' Weekly
Welsh Plant Breeding Station, Aberystwyth
Wimpole Hall Farm

FINDING OUT ABOUT

Modern Farming

Jeff Battersby and Dave Tilley

FRANKLIN WATTS
LONDON • NEW YORK • SYDNEY • TORONTO

Farming in Britain

Farming is one of the UK's most important industries and, although half the output is produced by only 12% of the total number of farmers, even those farming on a small scale have to be efficient to survive. Farming constantly changes as new ideas and advances in technology are made available.

There are over 240 000 farms in Britain (equivalent to one for every person living in Stoke on Trent) with an average size of 50 hectares (1 hectare is about the size of a football pitch). 690 000 people are employed on farms which represents 2.6% of the total workforce in Britain — about the same as the populations of Bradford, Brighton and Nottingham put together!

The land, the soil, and the climate vary a great deal throughout Britain and this has led to a number of different farming types and practices. The map opposite shows where the main types of farming can be found.

Types of Farming

- **Arable**
  Crops such as cereals, potatoes, sugar beet and vegetables

- **Livestock**
  Grassland with dairying and beef cattle and sheep

- **Mixed**
  Crops and livestock

- **Horticulture**
  Fruit and vegetables, bulbs, flowers and nursery plants often grown in glasshouses

- Pig and poultry farming takes place in buildings, so soil and climate are not important.

Types of Farming

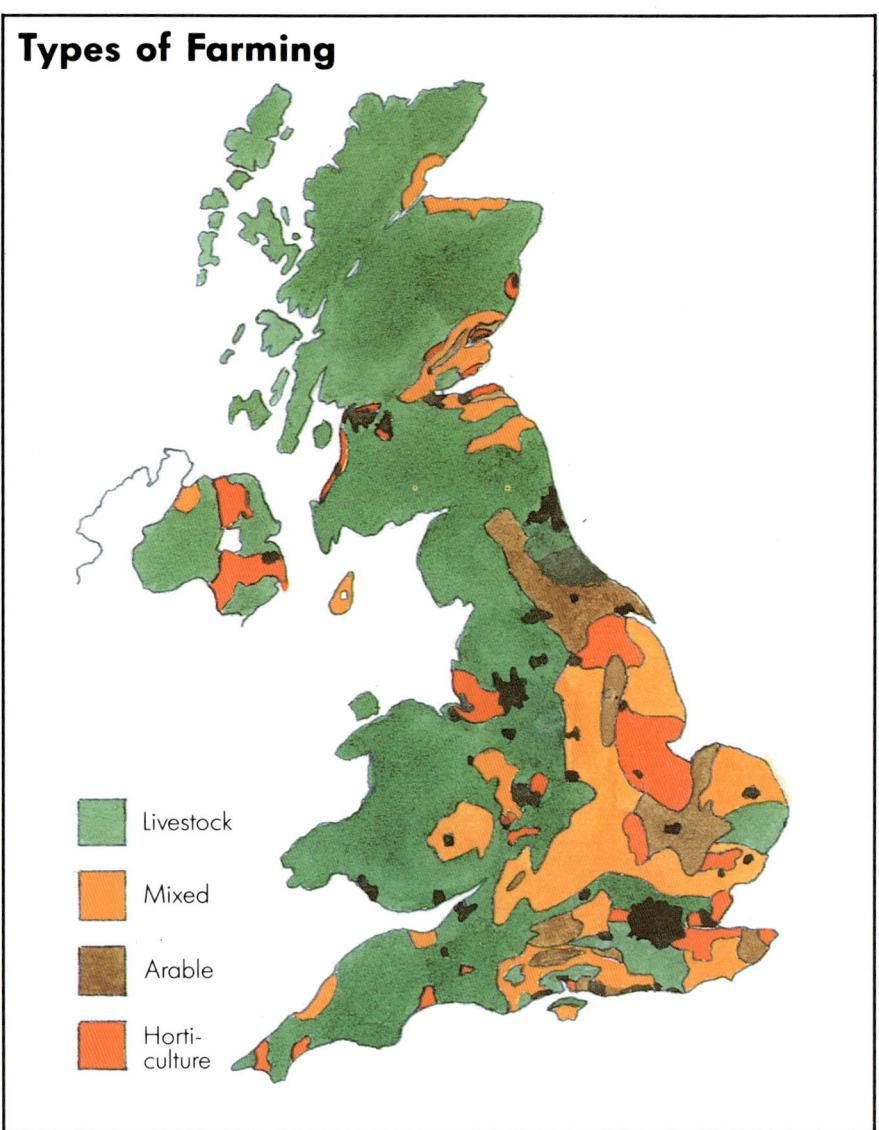

- Livestock
- Mixed
- Arable
- Horti-culture

What you might see on farms

Crops

Grass — the basic crop of the livestock farmer

Wheat — a basic part of our diet

Barley — another important cereal crop

Oilseed rape — which gives edible oil

Potatoes and sugar beet — the two most important root crops

Fruit and vegetables — such as cabbages, Brussels sprouts, onions, apples and raspberries

Animals

The most important farm animals are dairy and beef cattle, sheep, pigs and poultry.

Machines

Farming has become increasingly mechanised, and today there are few jobs that cannot be done by a machine.

WHAT YOU CAN DO

1 What are each of the crops listed used for? If you don't know try to find out.

2 What products do the animals give us?

3 Why is the tractor the most important farm machine?

The changing face of farming

The United Kingdom with a population of 56 million now produces much of its own food to be as self-sufficient as possible and to avoid the costs and insecurity of relying too much on imported food.

During the Second World War, when enemy action threatened our imported food supply, farmers were ordered to plough up grassland and grow more cereals and potatoes. After 1945, successive governments tried to secure food supplies and stabilise prices through a system of subsidies and grants: to guarantee a market for certain products, and to help pay for new equipment, buildings and drainage. Government policy influenced the farmer's choice of crops and animals and encouraged farmers to aim for maximum production.

When Britain joined the European Community (EC) in 1973, the system changed. The aim of the Common Agricultural Policy (CAP) is to guarantee the farmer an agreed price for certain commodities. To ensure this, EC authorities buy and store produce from farmers if the price falls below the agreed level. In theory these stocks of food are sold when there are shortages and prices are higher but, in practice, shortages rarely occur now and 'mountains' of cereals and butter and 'lakes' of wine and olive oil build up. What do you think the EC is doing about this problem? You might find some ideas as you read through the book.

Impact of Modern Farming Techniques

The vast increase in food production over the past 40 years has been made possible by:

- Crop varieties that give a higher yield; these are the result of selective breeding (a field of wheat now produces two and a half times as much grain as in 1945).
- animals that give more milk or meat because of improved breeding and feeding policies and techniques. (The average cow

now produces over twice as much milk as at the end of the war.)

- the increased use of fertilisers to enable the improved crop varieties to reach their full growth potential.
- the increased use of pesticides and herbicides to protect plants from pests, diseases and weeds.
- the development of mechanisation and automation.

Examples of the impact of technology on farming practice are very striking in the field of mechanisation. Machines can now do almost every job on the farm and fewer — though more highly skilled — workers are needed. Jobs like threshing grain, which used to rely on a large number of workers, have changed dramatically. A combine capable of harvesting a high-yielding crop of wheat can now cover up to 10 hectares a day with only one man at the controls, and one man can handle the milking of 120 cows or more in about two hours in an automated milking 'parlour'.

Changes in the countryside
The average size of a farm in Britain today is 50 hectares. This is much larger than in other EC countries, and five times larger than it was 40 years ago. Where possible, farmers have bought land from their neighbours to enlarge their farms to make them more economic and to enable larger and more expensive machines to be used economically. Some hedges have been removed, particularly on specialist arable farms where hedges are no longer required as fences or as shelter. However, most farmers try to combine good farming practice with care for the countryside. Many plant new trees, dig ponds and create places where wildlife can live.

Seventy five per cent of the population of the UK, or 40 million people, live in towns or cities of 10 000 inhabitants or more and this has had an impact on the surrounding countryside. But, in the age of the car, the effect is spread much farther as people who live in towns go to the countryside for their leisure and recreation.

Although the population has remained virtually the same for some years now, people tend to move from one part of the country to another, and from larger cities into smaller towns and villages. Farmland is being taken to build houses, roads and factories.

WHAT YOU CAN DO

Look at the two maps which show the quality of farmland and the areas where most people are found in Britain.

1 In which areas of Britain is there going to be the greatest pressure on farmland?

2 What quality of farmland has been taken to expand cities and to build roads?

3 What are the implications for farming as a result of these losses of land?

The trend towards an increase in the growth of large cities has slowed down since 1975 and this has taken some pressure off nearby farmland. At the same time, the production of food has increased enormously helped by modern farming techniques and more intensive methods of farming. So, perhaps we can afford to lose some farmland.

What do you think?

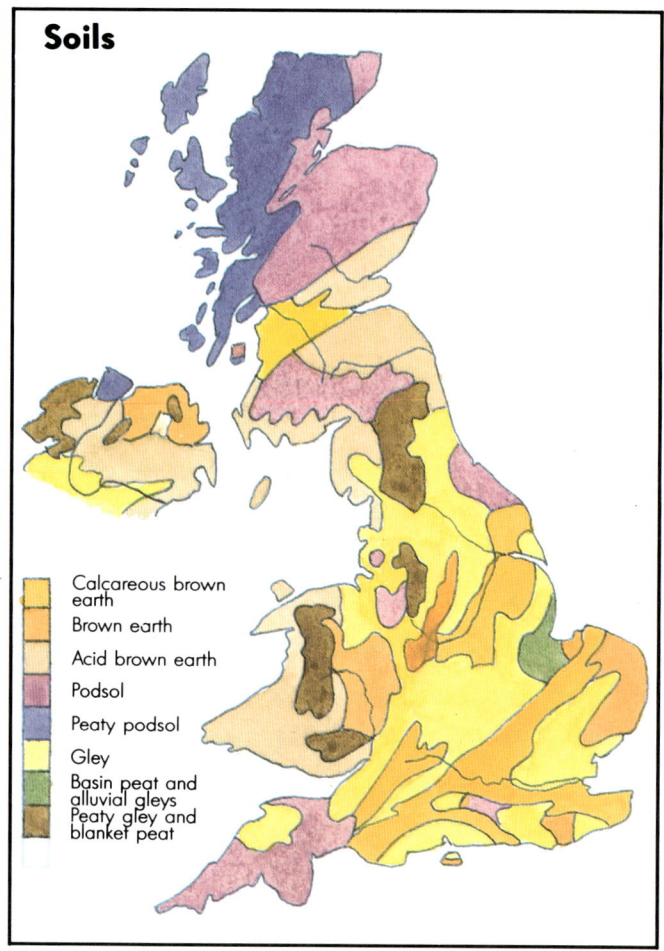

Soils

Calcareous brown earth
Brown earth
Acid brown earth
Podsol
Peaty podsol
Gley
Basin peat and alluvial gleys
Peaty gley and blanket peat

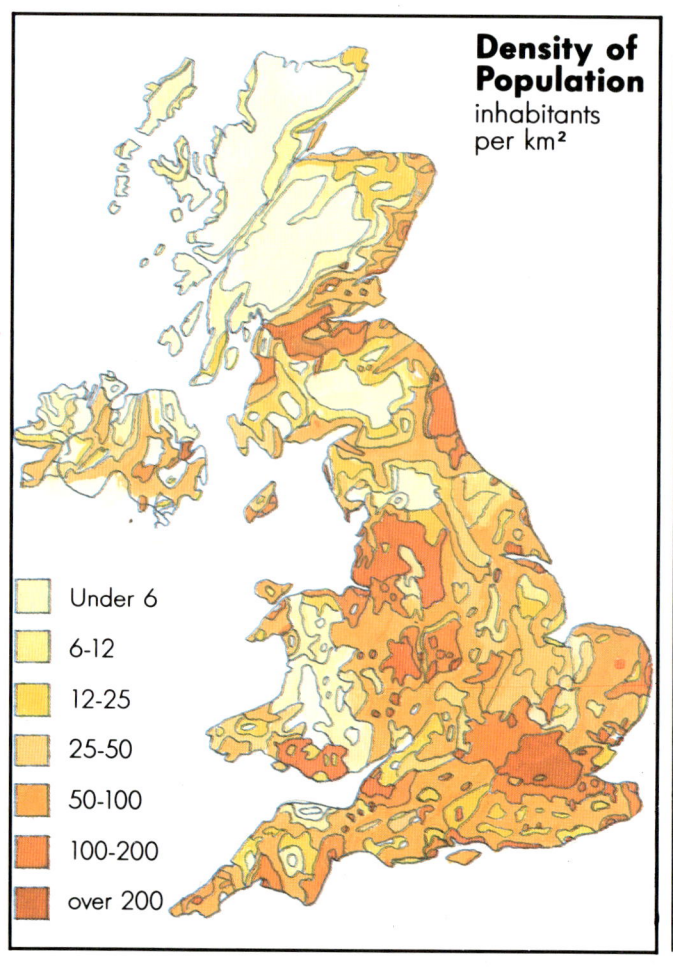

Density of Population
inhabitants per km²

Under 6
6-12
12-25
25-50
50-100
100-200
over 200

CASE STUDY

A motorway comes to the farm

The worst day in a farmer's life may come when he picks up the local paper and sees a map with a large blob on it covering his farm. It could mean a housing estate, a flyover or a motorway interchange. Such a moment came to Chiltern Farm when the plans for the new M40 to Oxford were published.

When the official plan arrived, it showed a major motorway junction in the centre of the farm, with another road built to bypass the village in which the farm was located. The whole scheme would take 12 hectares of the farm out of a total of 104 hectares. This does not sound very much but the proposal meant that the farm was split into eight parts, five of which were quite small parcels of land. It also meant long detours to get the farm machinery to the different fields and crossing the new bypass.

Chiltern Farm grew wheat on 35% of the land, barley on 45% and short-term grass on the other 20% of the land on which there was a 100 sow outdoor breeding unit, selling weaner pigs.

The day arrived when the bulldozers moved in, fences were broken down and dusty chalk was moved across the farm to build up high embankments to carry the new roads. The

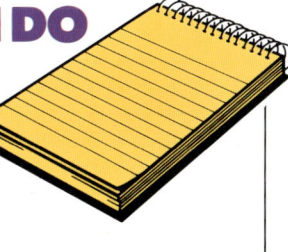

dust was terrible and flattened the crops. The pigs had to be sold at a time when pig prices were very low. For two years no livestock could be kept on the farm and profits slumped catastrophically.

WHAT YOU CAN DO

1 Imagine that you are the farmer at Chiltern Farm. What are the main problems that you have to face as a result of the motorway development?

2 What effects will the motorway construction have on your farm and the methods you use to farm it?

3 What might you try to do to improve your farm in the years to come?

3 The diversity of modern farming

Every farm has a unique location with advantages as well as disadvantages which have to be taken into account when deciding on the farming system to be followed. Farming practices have developed over a long period of time, shaping the type of farming and landscape in a particular place and helping to make the countryside what it is today.

In any location, the environment determines the seasonal rhythm of farm work. The physical characteristics of the land – its soil type, slope and aspect – are unchanging, but temperature and the availability of water can change from year to year, though their effects can sometimes be modified by the farmer.

Economic circumstances too can alter the farming pattern. Changes in government policy, in the price of basic inputs such as oil, in standards of living, in eating habits and in the size and location of the population, together with advances in technology, influence farming practice in different parts of Britain.

This chapter takes a look at five farms in different parts of Britain and shows how the farmers respond to the physical characteristics of their locations as well as to the economic conditions in which they find themselves.

The maps, as well as those on page 8 provide details of the physical environment.

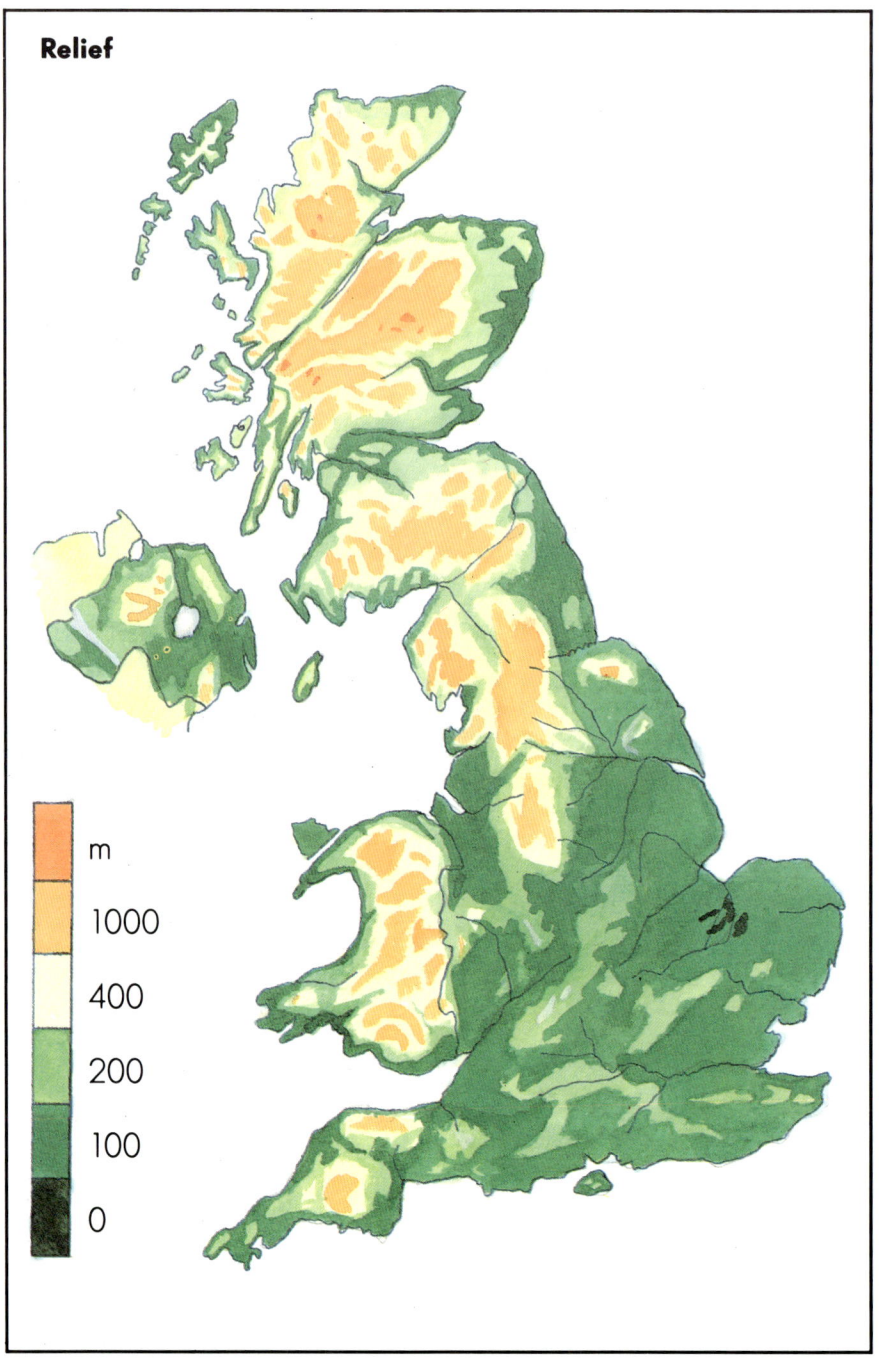

Relief

m	
1000	
400	
200	
100	
0	

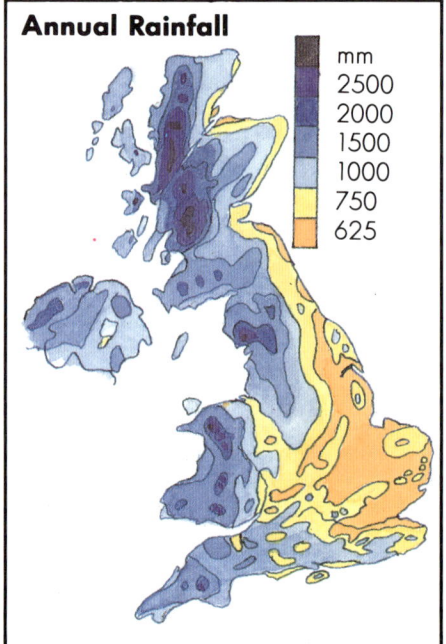

Annual Rainfall

mm	
2500	
2000	
1500	
1000	
750	
625	

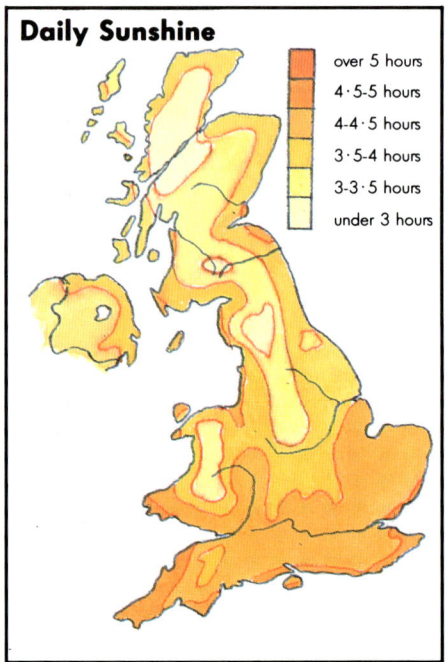

Daily Sunshine

over 5 hours
4·5-5 hours
4-4·5 hours
3·5-4 hours
3-3·5 hours
under 3 hours

CASE STUDY

An intensive arable farm in Lincolnshire
Yellow House Farm, Long Sutton, Spalding, Lincolnshire

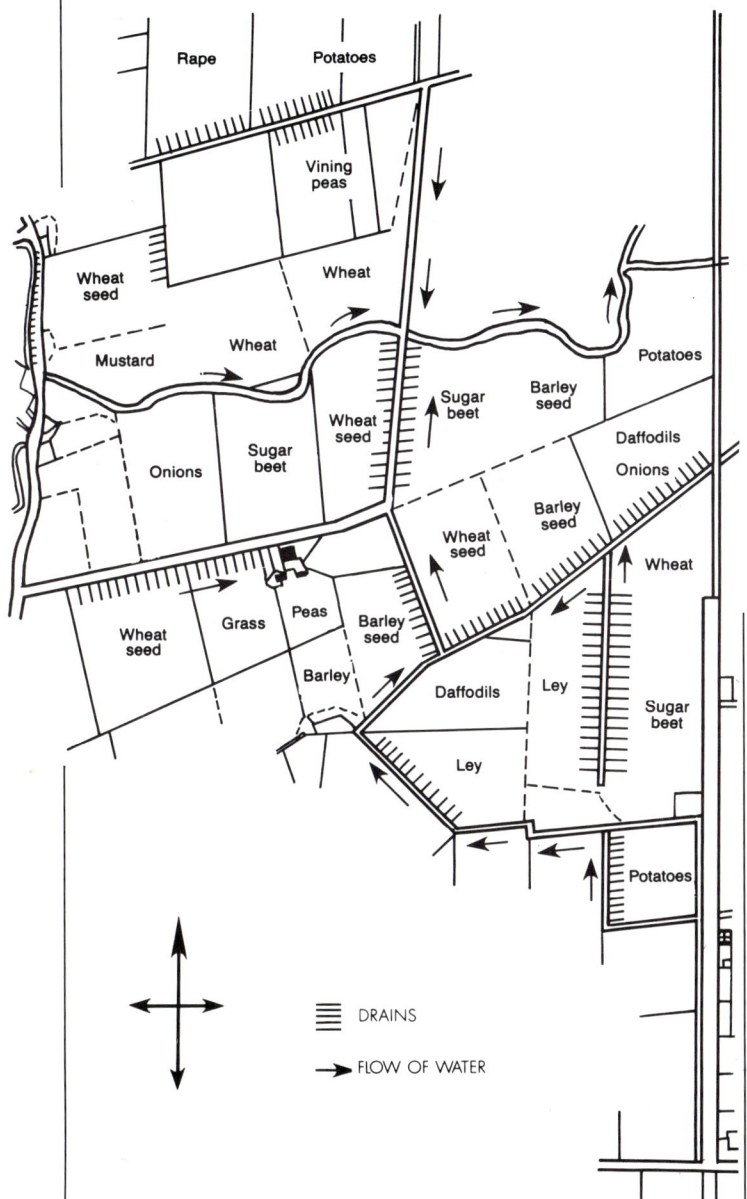

DRAINS

→ FLOW OF WATER

Farm facts

SIZE AND LAND USE: 177 ha: 156 ha under crops; 19 ha grass; 2 ha buildings

LIVESTOCK: 16 beef cows; 26 young cattle for fattening; 300 ewes

CROPS AND OUTPUT: Wheat (41 ha, 300 t), barley (23 ha, 130 t); sugar beet (24 ha, 1170 t); daffodils (14 ha, 180 t every other year); potatoes (28 ha, 850 t); vining peas (14 ha, 53 t); oilseed rape (9 ha, 33 t); onions (6 ha, 196 t); mustard (6 ha, 5 t); mangolds (0.6 ha, 30 t); grass (25 ha); woodland (0.4 ha)

WORKFORCE: 10 full-time and 4 part-time

MACHINERY AND BUILDINGS: 7 tractors; 1 combine harvester; 1 corn drill; 1 baler; 1 sprayer; 1 fertiliser spreader and 3 ploughs; 1 corn drier; storage for 380 t of grain and 400 t of straw

Yellow House Farm is an intensive arable farm situated on rich silt soils in a flat area 1.5 m below sea-level near the Wash. The total rainfall is only 550 mm (22 in) and it is very exposed to cold north winds in the spring. There are no hedges or walls separating the fields, but dykes which drain water from the land act as boundaries.

The usual crop rotation is peas—potatoes—wheat then either sugar beet, oilseed rape or ley grass. The onions, mustard, mangolds and daffodils are fitted in as convenient.

All the barley straw and two-thirds of the wheat straw is baled as it is needed by the livestock and is used to protect the potatoes and onions. How might livestock use the straw? Why is it used to protect the potatoes and onions?

CASE STUDY

An upland sheep farm in Cumbria
Raisbeck, Orton, Penrith, Cumbria

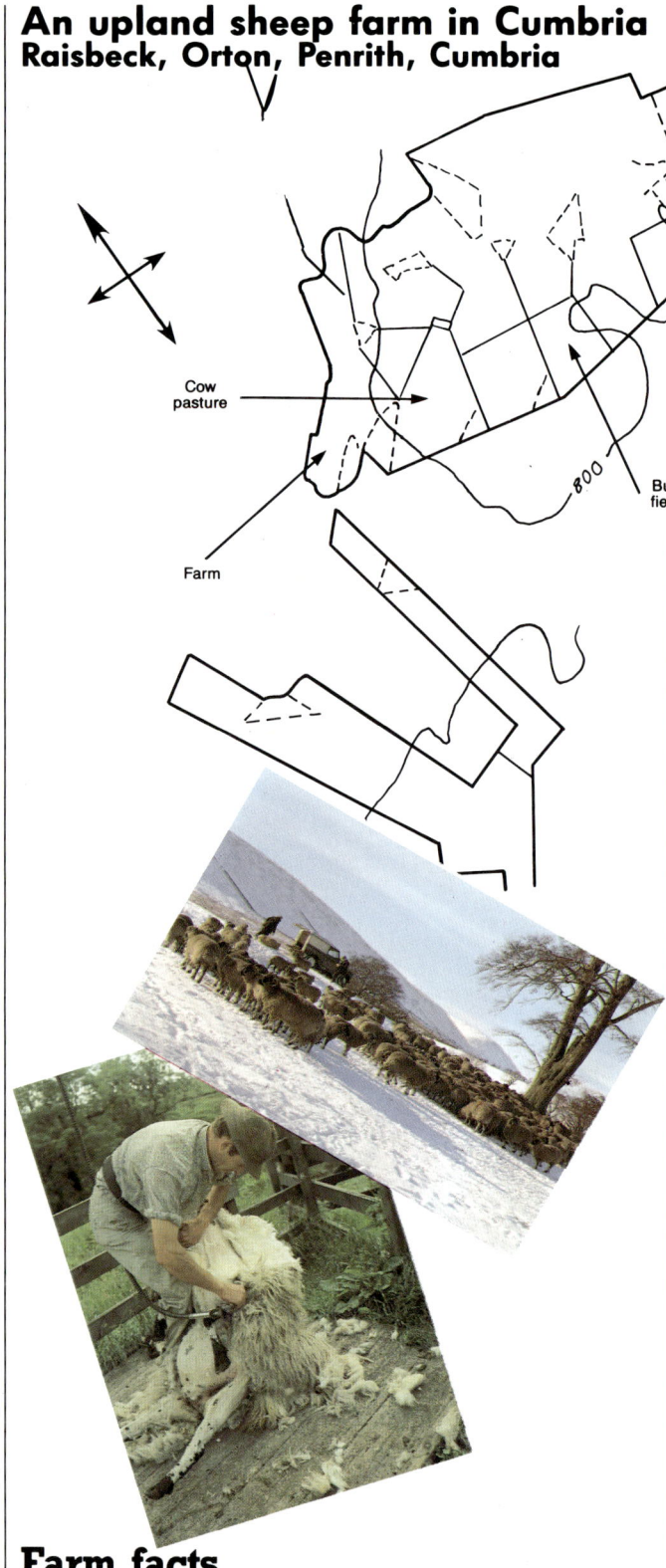

Nature reserve

Cow pasture

Bull field

Farm

Raisbeck has been farmed by the same family for over 200 years. The farm is on a limestone soil, receives 1650 mm (65 in) of rain each year, lies between 228–305 m (750–1000 ft) above sea-level in an exposed area of land which experiences very cold winters. The fields are divided up by dry stone walls and streams provide water for the stock in every field.

The flock of 1035 breeding ewes produced 1505 lambs last year, which were fattened for market at five months old when they weighed 19 kg each. About 300 ewes are sold each year to lowland farmers for further breeding. Lambing takes place in April, after the worst of the winter. Shearing is in June/July when 2000 kg of wool are produced from the whole flock.

No cereal crops can be grown in such a harsh climate but swedes are grown to provide winter feed for the cattle and the sheep. Grass is also grown for winter feed as either silage or hay.

70 t of fertiliser are used each year – mainly in the form of phosphate to encourage the growth of clover. Lime is also applied at frequent intervals to correct the acidity in the soil.

The farmer is attempting to improve the environment of the farm and has planted a number of small woodland areas and shelter belts as well as creating three ponds. The wildlife in the area has certainly benefited with buzzards, owls and curlews now nesting on the farm. A nature trail is being planned for use by the general public. Already the farmer sells day tickets for fishing in his trout-filled ponds in an attempt to supplement his income.

Farm facts
SIZE AND LAND USE: 283 ha: 279 ha in permanent grass and 4 ha in crops
LIVESTOCK: 1035 breeding ewes; 95 beef suckler cows; 116 young beef stock; 2 bulls
CROPS AND OUTPUT: Swedes (4 ha, 300 t); grass (8 ha, 900 t silage + 60 t hay)
WORKFORCE: 3 full-time and some part-time help at lambing
MACHINERY: 5 tractors; 1 baler; 1 sprayer; 1 plough; 1 fertiliser spreader

CASE STUDY

A West Country dairy farm
Bridge Farm, West Bradley, Glastonbury, Somerset

Farm facts

SIZE AND LAND USE: 132 ha: 110 ha in grass (90 ha permanent pasture and 20 in leys); 12 ha barley; 5 ha cider apple orchard; 3 ha forage turnips

LIVESTOCK: 130 Friesian cows; 167 heifers; 20–24 male calves for beef, 30 breeding ewes

OUTPUT: Milk quota for the farm is 727 778 litres a year and, in 1985, 709 800 litres were produced, a yield of 5854 litres per cow. All of the milk is sold to make into farmhouse cheese. Most of the barley (average 5.8 t per ha) is sold to a local pig farmer. The apples (on average 40 t a year) are sold.

WORKFORCE: 4 full-time; 1 part-time

MACHINERY AND BUILDINGS: 6 tractors; a plough; a sprayer; a baler; a forage harvester; a fertiliser spreader; a 14/14 herringbone milking parlour; Dutch barns and a silo with capacity for 1450 t of grass silage

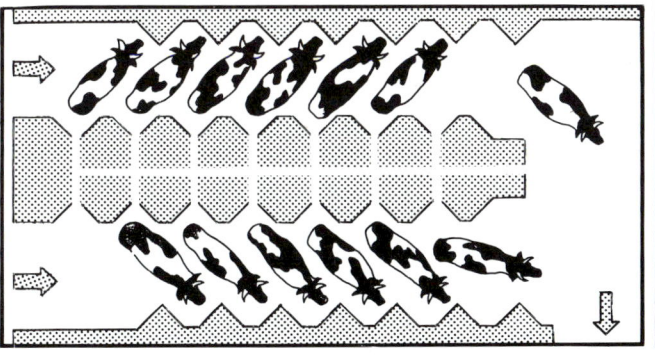

Bridge Farm lies just off the flat Somerset plain 30 m above sea-level. The soil is heavy, and with a rainfall of 750 mm (30 in) it is an ideal farm for growing grass. The fields are quite small averaging 4 ha, and the grass is heavily fertilised to produce high yields for summer grazing and winter feed. There are 130 cubicles for the cows and 70 for the heifers, and three strawed yards for wintering the rest of the young stock and beef cattle.

A computer has been installed in the farm office for recording the performance of the herd and for handling the accounts.

Barley is now grown because the straw is invaluable for bedding and feeding animals, and the grain is a useful cash crop and a good feed for the young stock. The sheep flock, though small, is valuable since good prices can be obtained for the pedigree ram lambs sold for breeding.

CASE STUDY

A mixed cereal and dairy farm
Friar's Court, Clanfield, Oxfordshire

Map labels: Grass, Wood, Grass, Wheat, Barley, Grass, Wheat, Wheat, Barley, Wheat, Grass, Grass, Grass, Grass, Barley, Oilseed Rape, Barley, Wheat, Barley, Lake, Wheat, Wheat, Barley, Wheat, Wheat

Farm facts

SIZE AND LAND USE: 228 ha: 143 ha under crops; 11.5 ha woodland

LIVESTOCK: 60 Friesian cows; 30 heifers; 70 calves for beef

CROPS AND OUTPUT: wheat (70 ha, 450 t); barley (56 ha, 300 t); oilseed rape (11 ha, 20 t); grass silage (500 t); hay (85 t); kale (6 ha); milk (350 000 litres)

WORKFORCE: 4 full-time; 1 part-time

MACHINERY AND BUILDINGS: 4 tractors; 1 combine harvester; 1 forage harvester; 1 baler; 1 corn drill; 1 sprayer; 1 fertiliser spreader; 1 corn dryer with storage for 750 t; 1 8/8 herringbone milking parlour

Friar's Court is situated on very flat land adjoining the Thames. Two-thirds of it lies on quite light, blackish river loam, and the rest on medium loam or Oxford clay. The average rainfall is only 600 mm (24 in). It is a mixed farm, roughly two-thirds being in arable crops and a third in temporary grass. The farmer uses a lot of nitrogen for the dairy grass but is hoping to reduce this.

All the barley straw and half the wheat straw is baled for use by the livestock. 3000 bales are sold, and the other half of the wheat straw is burned on the field.

The farmer is very involved with conservation and recreation. An official Caravan Club site and a licensed caravan rally site have been provided in a field next to the river. The farmer intends to plant a hectare of land with willow trees which will help wildlife and provide rapidly growing tree biomass.

There are two crop rotations, the first consisting of two cereal crops, followed by three years ley, with the kale cash crop put in in the final year. The second rotation consists of four to six years cereals, followed by two years ley, or oilseed rape.

Cereal	**1**	Cereal
Cereal	**2**	Cereal
Ley	**3**	Cereal
Ley	**4**	Cereal
Ley	**5**	Ley or Rape
Kale	**6**	Ley or Rape

CASE STUDY

A specialist cereal farm in Essex
New Hall, Little Wigborough, Colchester, Essex

Crops are wheat and rape. Note the position of the rivers

Farm facts

SIZE AND LAND USE: 203 ha: 192.5 ha arable; 6.5 ha woodland; 4 ha rough grass
CROPS AND OUTPUT: 800 t high quality bread wheat; 90 t lower quality feed wheat at an average yield of 6.25 t per ha; 138 t of oilseed rape at 3.6 t per ha (figures for 1985)
WORKFORCE: 3 full-time
MACHINERY AND BUILDINGS: 6 working tractors; 1 combine harvester; 3 ploughs; 1 corn drill; 3 sprayers; 1 fertiliser spreader; storage for 2000 t of grain

New Hall Farm is situated on a very heavy clay soil at an altitude varying from just below sea-level to 10 m above and with an average rainfall of only 500 mm (20 in). The whole of the farm is arable land with only two crops — wheat and oilseed rape. Over the past 45 years the farmer has given up growing barley, beans, peas and grass and the keeping of cows, pigs, sheep, poultry and turkeys in favour of the present ultra-simple system. All the machinery is overhauled and maintained by the farm staff in the winter and the machinery costs are very low for a farm of this type.

All the accounts are computerised and the costs of producing a crop are accurately available at any time during the production process. Attention to detail is important; for example, all drains are carefully inspected each year and repaired if necessary, and the closest watch kept on the level of the inputs.

In spite of his specialised system of farming, the farmer considers conservation highly important. He has planted trees and excavated a lake.

The farming year

Some of the jobs done on farms during the different seasons of the year are shown on the farming calendar.

	OCT	NOV	DEC	JAN	FEB	MAR	APR	MAY	JUN	JUL	AUG	SEP
Cultivation and cropping	Ploughing. Sow Winter Barley and Wheat. Harvest Potatoes and Sugar Beet.	Sowing finished.	Ditching and Hedging.		Early Fertiliser to wheat.	Sow Spring barley and Spring Oats. Top Dress with Fertiliser. Plant early Potatoes, and Sugar Beet. Spraying for Weeds, Fungus.		Spray Cereals and Roots for Weeds and Diseases.	Lift early Potatoes.	Harvest Winter Barley and Oilseed Rape.	Harvest Wheat and Barley. Plough and sow Oilseed Rape.	Sow Winter Barley.
Fruit and vegetables	Harvest last apples and pears.	Harvest grapes.			Prune fruit trees.			Spray for insects and fungus.	Harvest strawberries, raspberries and other soft fruit.			Harvest apples and pears.
			Vegetables planted and harvested in succession all year round; containerised plants and trees, and glasshouse flowers in production all through the year.									
Grassland					Apply early Fertiliser.	Fertiliser for Silage and Hay. Grazing		Cut Silage.	Make Hay.	2nd Cut Silage.		
Dairy herd	Autumn Calving. Silage Feeding.	Cows Housed.	Serve cows for Autumn Calving.		Spring Calving		Cows out to Grass. Calves to Grass.		Serve Cows for Spring Calving.			Autumn Calving starts.
Beef cattle	Autumn Calving. Cattle for Finishing into yards. Wean Spring born Calves.	Cows and Calves may be housed.	Finished cattle to market. Autumn Calvers to Bull.			Spring Calves born.	Housed Cows and Calves to Grass.		Serve Cows for Spring Calving. Wean Autumn Calves.			Wean Spring born Calves.
Sheep	Ewes to Ram for March Lambing Dipping		Some ewes housed for winter.	Early lambing starts.		Main Lambing period. Housed ewes to Grass.	Early lambs to market. Shearing.		Dipping		Spring born lambs weaned, and sold finished, or as stores. Early ewes to Ram.	
Pigs and poultry	Some farm jobs go on all the time, including pig and poultry production, with peaks of activity but independent of the seasons.											

WHAT YOU CAN DO

Compare the different jobs carried out on an arable farm with those on a sheep farm. In what ways are they influenced by the weather?

Like all other industries, farming has a system made up of inputs, which can be physical or human, processes such as growing crops or rearing animals, and outputs or farm products which are available for sale.

The diagram shows a system of inputs and outputs for a dairy farm. Can you think of other inputs? Try to explain what it shows and make similar 'models' for the case studies in this book or for a farm which you know.

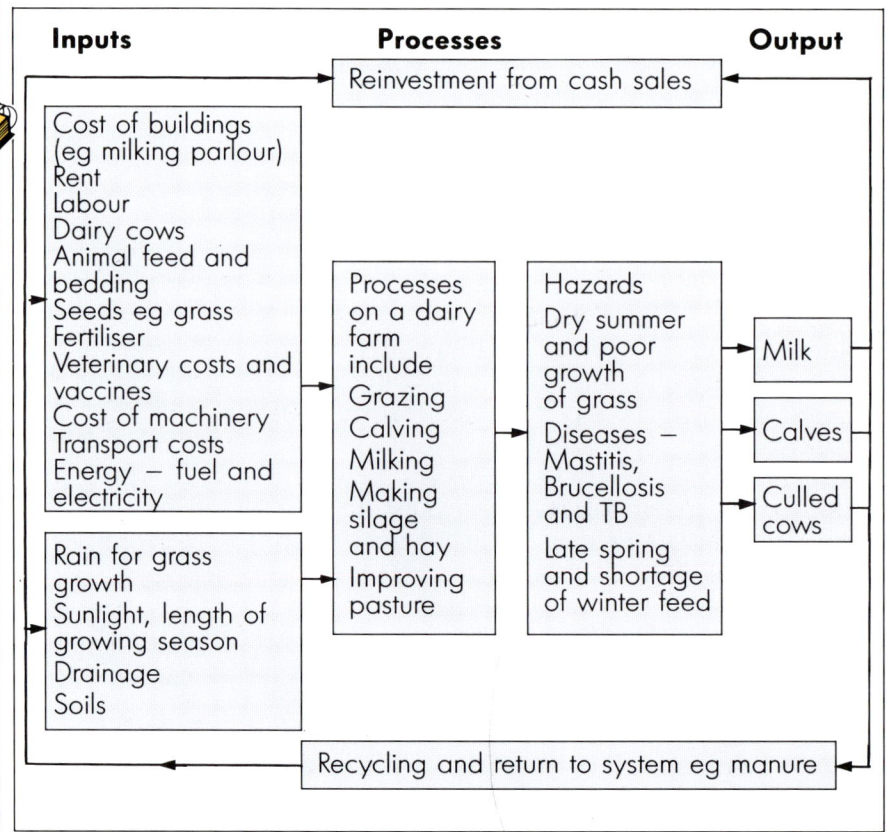

Inputs — Processes — Output

Reinvestment from cash sales

Inputs:
Cost of buildings (eg milking parlour)
Rent
Labour
Dairy cows
Animal feed and bedding
Seeds eg grass
Fertiliser
Veterinary costs and vaccines
Cost of machinery
Transport costs
Energy — fuel and electricity

Rain for grass growth
Sunlight, length of growing season
Drainage
Soils

Processes on a dairy farm include
Grazing
Calving
Milking
Making silage and hay
Improving pasture

Hazards
Dry summer and poor growth of grass
Diseases — Mastitis, Brucellosis and TB
Late spring and shortage of winter feed

Output:
Milk
Calves
Culled cows

Recycling and return to system eg manure

4 Aspects of modern farming

Early people obtained food from wild plants and animals. As hunter−gatherers they hunted animals for meat and gathered edible fruits, leaves, stems and roots. This primitive lifestyle was fine because the human population was small and it had little impact on wild plants and animals.

But, as populations increased and knowledge developed, this way of life was replaced by a more settled agriculture. About 10 000 years ago people started to select and cultivate nutritious plants and harvest them, and to herd and domesticate animals in enclosures. Eventually, they began to grow enough food to sell to other people. To do this, they cut down trees, cleared and ploughed the land and adapted the environment.

Farming systems have evolved throughout the ages to meet the needs of the people. Today's more intensive farming methods have developed in response to the demands of a large population for a varied and healthy diet.

WHAT YOU CAN DO

In 1798 Thomas Malthus suggested that the population of the earth would outstrip its food supply. Do you think his prediction has come true?

Crops

Although there are many thousands of plant species in the world, few are cultivated to produce food. The main crops grown in Britain are:

Grass 70% of all agricultural land in the UK is in grass and rough grazings. Grass is one of Britain's greatest natural assets. Although *we* cannot eat grass, cattle and sheep are able to convert it into meat and milk.

Cereals The main cereals are wheat and barley; oats are now only grown, to a limited extent, in the West and North. The cereal grain or seed contains protein, starches, vitamin B and fibre.

Legumes These are plants like beans and peas. The seeds are fairly high in protein, and the roots have nodules which contain bacteria that convert nitrogen from the air to nitrates, valuable for soil fertility.

Wheat

Oats

Barley

Potatoes

Root crops and tubers Plants such as potatoes, sugar beet, carrots and swedes are all important field crops as sugars and starches are stored in their swollen roots.

Forage crops These are crops such as kale and cabbage grown for their leaves, which are used as fodder for livestock.

Oilseed rape Oilseed rape is grown for its seed from which the oil is extracted.

In 1985, over 22 million tonnes of grain were produced and nearly 15 million tonnes of potatoes and sugar beet. How do we use all this produce?

Look at these simple food chains:

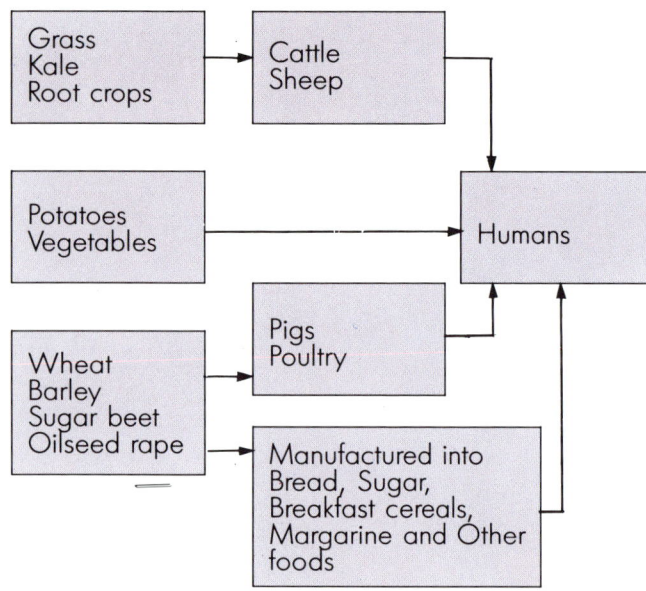

WHAT YOU CAN DO

1 Make a list of other food products that are produced from these crops and animals.

2 Name three crops that are grown in your area. How are they used in the production of food?

3 Look at the labels of some different food products that you use at home. Write down the ingredients and (1) try to find out which crops were used to make them and (2) list them in the following table.

Food Product	Crop	Protein	Fat	Carbohydrate	Fibre	Additives and colouring
Breakfast cereal						
Crisps						
Sausages						
Frozen peas						
Tinned carrots						
Jam						

How do plants grow?

Farmers depend on a complex biological process for all the crops they grow and harvest. Healthy plants will be produced only if the soil contains enough nutrients. If we were to rely on the soil's nutrient 'bank' alone, yields would be poor and the 'bank' would be gradually reduced to a point where crops would not be worth growing. So farmers use fertilisers to boost the soil's own nutrient supply.

Germination, growth, pollination and fruiting

WHAT YOU CAN DO

1 Using the illustration to help you, explain in your own words how plants grow.

2 Find out what the main 'ingredients' of fertilisers are and where they come from.

Plant breeding and improvement

For hundreds of years farmers tried to breed better crops by saving the best seed from the best crops at harvest. But this was not very successful. Now, the use of genetics (the science of heredity) is the key to producing better quality plant varieties and strains. Plant breeders concentrate on 'fixing' specific characteristics found in pure-bred strains and then inter-cross these with other strains selected for different qualities. Hybrids, produced by crossing two in-bred strains, also show a vigour which is not present in either of the parents.

In some cases, modern plant breeding has helped the increase of production by as much as 250%. The improved strains of rice now used in developing countries are an example of this so-called 'green revolution'.

Look at this wheat breeding programme:

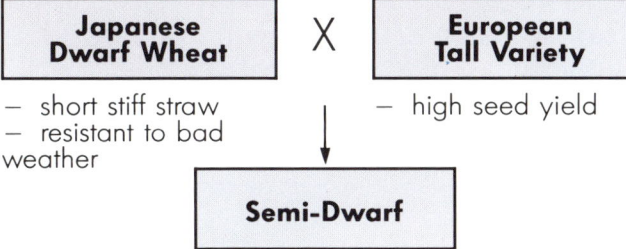

Japanese Dwarf Wheat	X	European Tall Variety
– short stiff straw – resistant to bad weather		– high seed yield

Semi-Dwarf

What advantages will the semi-dwarf wheat have over its parents?

Horticultural crops

Commercial horticulture includes glasshouse production, the growing of fruit and vegetables and the production of shrubs and flowers.

The weather in Britain can be unpredictable. Summers can be wet and cold as well as very hot; winters, too, can be mild or severe. Horticultural crops are easily damaged by wind, temperature and rainfall. Farmers and growers have therefore developed systems which attempt to improve artificially the environment in which crops grow.

Glasshouse production

Tomatoes, lettuces and out of season vegetables, flowers and pot plants are all grown successfully in commercial glasshouses.

Vegetables

Vegetable growing has tended to move out into the fields on a farm scale because the high costs of hand labour have led to the use of machines which need larger areas for working.

Fruit

Much top (tree) fruit and soft fruit (grown on a bush, cane or low-growing plant) is grown successfully in Britain.

Top fruit Apples, pears, plums and cherries are grown in orchards in warmer parts of the country. English dessert and cooking varieties of apples such as Cox's Orange Pippins and Bramleys do well in our climate. Varieties suitable for cider making are mostly found in the West country.

Soft fruit such as strawberries, raspberries and red and blackcurrants are grown fairly extensively. Eastern Scotland, where you might think the weather was unsuitable, is renowned for its raspberries.

Shrubs and flowers Garden centres sell a variety of seeds, flowers, pot plants, bedding out plants, shrubs and trees.

Imported varieties Out of season tomatoes, new potatoes and cucumbers, as well as seeds and spices, are all imported from hotter countries such as Cyprus and the Canary Islands.

WHAT YOU CAN DO

1 Look at the photograph of vegetables. How many of them can you name?

2 In how many different ways might they be used?

3 What other imported fruit and vegetables do we eat? Where do they come from?

4 What problems do you think the fruit and vegetable grower faces in this country?

CASE STUDY

A fruit farm in the Vale of Evesham
Cotswold Orchards, Broadway, Worcestershire

Farm facts

SIZE AND LAND USE: 30 ha: 25 ha apples, 5 ha plums

CROPS AND OUTPUT: 7 varieties of apples, eating varieties such as Cox's Orange, Lord Lambourne or Egremont Russet (12t per ha), and cookers, such as Bramleys (20t per ha); 2 varieties of plums, Victoria and Marjorie Seedling (12t per ha)

WORKFORCE: 4 full-time; 8 part-time. Up to 20 casual workers are taken on for the harvest

MACHINERY AND BUILDINGS: 5 tractors; 2 sprayers; a forklift; bin handling equipment and a mower. There is a packhouse with grading line, bin tipper and polisher. Stores for 200 t of apples and a controlled atmosphere storage shed for 150 t to keep apples till February

This holding is situated on a sandy/clay soil, which can be rather wet in winter but holds moisture in the summer, with a rainfall of 70 mm (28 in) a year. Like many fruit farms it has become very specialised, and now grows only apples and plums.

All picking is done by hand, the fruit being packed for marketing to wholesalers or into supermarkets. It is also sold through the farm shop.

Very little machinery is needed and the holding is labour-intensive. However, expensive storage is needed and the cost of maintaining a quality product is high because of the cost of the spraying programme.

It can also be a high-risk operation, as good weather at pollination time is crucial.

An intensive glasshouse holding in Sussex
Old Barn Nursery, North Mundham, Chichester, Sussex

Farm facts
SIZE AND LAND USE: 3 ha, of which 0.7 ha is under glass
CROPS AND OUTPUT: winter lettuce; celery and tomatoes (1986 output – 210 000 lettuces; tomatoes 190–240 t per ha in May; 100–120 t per ha late planting)
WORKFORCE: 3 full-time; 2 part-time; some students are taken on in the summer
MACHINERY AND BUILDINGS: 2 tractors and trailers; a rotary cultivator; a lettuce planter; a celery grader; a sprayer; a spray tank; a peat blocker; 4 glasshouses; a packhouse and a cold-store

Glasshouse production has become increasingly specialised in the past 15 years. Here, only three crops are now grown, winter lettuce, celery and tomatoes. Celery is grown both in the house and outside. The advantage of this simple system is that each crop is grown in its natural season, the houses are in use throughout the year, and not too much artificial heating is required.

The soil is analysed before planting to ensure that the right fertilisers are used. All the soil is sterilised once every two years to eliminate fungal root or stem diseases.

A very close watch is also kept for greenfly and whitefly attacks, especially on tomatoes, and spraying is then used to eliminate them.

The lettuce and celery is graded and packed at home and sold to supermarket chains. The tomatoes are packed at a central co-operative packing station from which they also go to supermarkets.

How can plants be protected from the weather?

Not very much can be done to protect crops from the effects of wind, frost, snow or very heavy rain. Cereal crops can be flattened by a storm, though the introduction of short-strawed varieties has lessened the risk. Fruit trees are at risk from late frosts, though their siting on a slope can minimise the danger of low-lying frost pockets.

Crops can suffer seriously in a dry summer, especially those on light soils. If a good water supply is available, it can often pay a grower to irrigate. Large mobile sprinklers are usually used.

Protection from pests, diseases and weeds

Pests still destroy an estimated 30% of the world's agricultural production. In Britain, farmers lose millions of pounds each year from the effects of fungi in particular.

Insecticides protect crops from insects such as greenfly, weevils, codling moths, other larvae and caterpillars.
Herbicides control or kill the weeds which compete with the crop for soil nutrients and space.
Fungicides control moulds, rots and blights. These are still a major problem causing wastage and spoiling of crops, either while they are growing or when they are in store.

Farmers must apply all pesticides with great care and in the right concentrations. Chemicals are carefully tested before they are sold and, provided they are applied according to the instruction on the label, workers, wildlife, other people in the area, and consumers should be in no danger.

Farmers can help to reduce both pests and weeds by a rotation of crops and careful cultivations, but selective breeding and chemicals will still be the farmer's main line of defence for the foreseeable future.

WHAT YOU CAN DO

1 Look at the pictures: from what, in each case, is the farmer protecting his crop?

2 Can you think of any other ways of protecting crops from the weather?

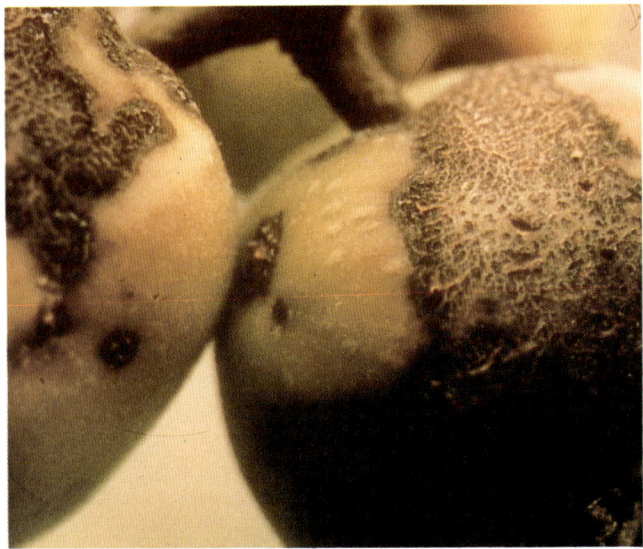

The growing, harvesting and marketing of crops

The busiest times on a farm are sowing and harvest.

Planting time can be anxious because the quick and efficient establishment of a crop is vital for good growth and final yield.

Harvest is a worrying time because the crop has been grown and the farmer does not want to see it spoiled by bad weather which reduces yield and quality.

Quality products are expected by merchants and consumers:

- Farmers will not get a good price for a crop such as wheat for milling, or barley for malting if the grain is in poor condition. Mouldy, shrivelled, cracked or over-dried grain all reduce the price very considerably.

- Wheat for milling must have a high protein content, and barley must be plump, starchy and a good colour.

- Potatoes, tomatoes, apples and other fruit must be undamaged and free from blemishes.

Machines on the farm

Today's machines have come a long way from the heavy, clumsy plough with its team of oxen used in the Middle Ages. Powerful tractors, seven-furrow reversible ploughs, wide implements, highly complex and expensive harvesters, pickers, sprayers and drills have all made farm work easier and more efficient. The expertise and training of the operators is now an important part of the job. Because of the cost of the machinery and the skill needed to use it, farmers sometimes use outside contractors.

WHAT YOU CAN DO

Look at the photographs and illustrations of some of the machines that are used in modern farming:

Try to work out what each machine or implement does.

Do you think there are risks involved in relying so heavily on machines? What would happen if there was a shortage of oil?

Write a brief paragraph describing how the combine harvester works.

What is the cost?

Typical costs (1986 prices):

Small tractor	£9 000
Large tractor	£20 000
Combine harvester	£48 000
Pick up baler	£4 800
Potato planter	£3 500
Forage harvester	£6 000
Seed drill	£4 000
Hedge cutter	£3 200
Fertiliser spreader	£2 200
Land Rover	£10 000

Apart from the expense of purchasing a range of machines, running and depreciation costs are also high.

The annual costs for a small tractor (costing about £9 000) might be:

Depreciation	£1 125
Tax and insurance	£94
Average repairs and maintenance	£720
Fuel/oil	£1 000
Total	£2 939

You can see that, if a farmer needs a range of machines and equipment, he will have to spend a lot of money.

Would one farmer need all the machines mentioned in the list? Which machines would he be most likely to use on contract?

Servicing and maintenance

Machines are often used for long hours, sometimes on wet, muddy fields or on light, dusty soil and in varying temperatures. Some are highly specialised and are only used for a few weeks in the year. They are then stored, inactive, until they are wanted again. Farm workers should be able to carry out routine maintenance work themselves before the next season.

Machines of the future

All machines have become larger and more sophisticated over the years. This trend is likely to continue. Rapid developments in technology and in the application of micro-processors could mean that machines will be programmed and controlled by on-board computers, in much the same way as auto-pilots in aeroplanes. Already, tractors can be programmed to do certain work by remote control, but considerable operational problems remain.

Buildings on the farm

Buildings can be
- traditional, but often inconvenient today
- modern and functional
- old, but adapted to suit modern needs.

WHAT YOU CAN DO

1 Look at the pictures of the farm buildings – old and new. Decide what the buildings are made of, what they are used for, and whether they are old, new or adapted.

2 Most farm buildings and the machines used in them rely on electricity. What do you think would happen if there was a power cut?

Look at the pictures and, using the chart below as a guide, suggest the advantages and disadvantages of each set of buildings by ticking the appropriate column.

	NEW	OLD
Ventilation		
Ease of working in building		
Ease/cost of maintenance		
Safety standards		
Attractiveness/landscaping		

Livestock

Livestock are the backbone of Britain's agricultural industry. Dairy and beef cattle, pigs, sheep and poultry provide us with meat, milk, eggs and a range of other produce.

Livestock are kept on both upland and lowland farms. Many farms in the uplands breed sheep and beef cattle for rearing and for fattening in the lowlands. Dairy herds are found mainly in specialist grassland areas in the West and also on mixed farms in other parts of the country. Pigs and poultry are mostly kept in intensive units wherever it may be economic or convenient.

Cattle

Cattle are kept either for milk or beef. One of the breeds in the photographs is French.

Which is it?

Hereford (beef)

Friesian

Jersey (dairy)

Charolais (beef)

Dairy Cattle The dairy breed most often seen in Britain is the Friesian. Like all mammals, the dairy cow produces milk to feed her calf. However, as the result of selective breeding over the years, she produces far more milk than the calf needs, especially as most calves are taken away and bucket fed.

To give milk, a cow must first become pregnant and produce a calf. The cows are served by the bull or – as is more common today – AI is used, that is, sperm are introduced by artificial insemination. This is convenient because sperm from a high quality bull can be collected and stored for long periods in a deep freeze, and any suitable cow can be inseminated.

Calving Dairy farmers generally aim either for autumn or spring calving. In spring calving, milk is produced mainly from grass, but the price is lower. Autumn calving earns a higher winter milk price because less milk is produced at this time, but costs of production are higher. Why do you think this is?

Look at the graph which illustrates the milk production pattern. Lactation, following calving, lasts for about 10 months – approximately 305 days – but then the cow must have a rest before she has another calf.

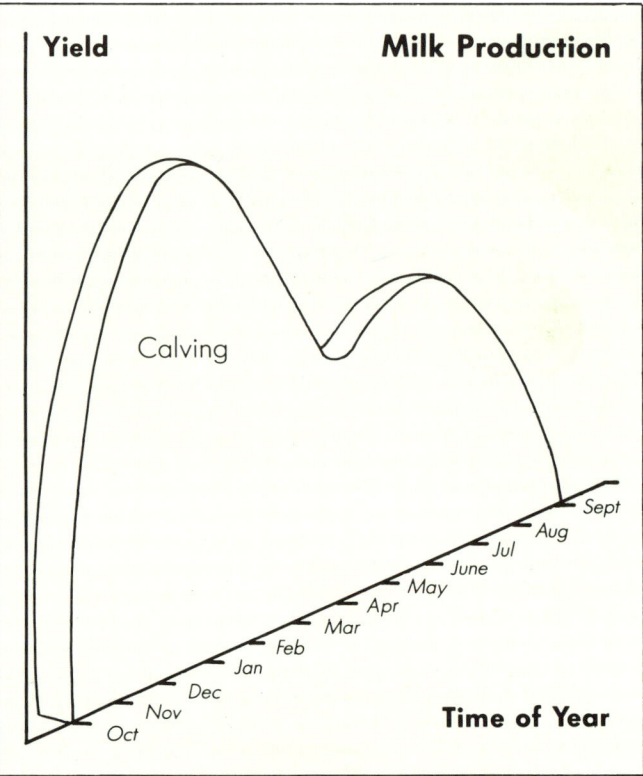

Why does milk production go up again in April and May?

26

Beef Cattle Calves are reared and fattened for meat. The beef we can buy comes from three different sources:

1 From breeds of cows, specially selected for high quality beef production, which suckle their calves. The herds are mostly kept in upland areas not suitable for dairying.

2 From the dairy herd: bull calves and heifer calves not needed as replacements for the dairy herd, often coming from some of the lower yielding cows in the herd, mated with a beef bull. This produces calves that fatten quickly. (See diagram.)

3 Cows that are culled (removed) from the herd, which can provide beef of reasonable quality if not too old.

Beef from the Dairy Herd

Friesian cow (Dairy)	X	Hereford bull (Beef)

↓

Cross-bred calf showing white face of Hereford and good meat quality

The cross-bred calf inherits the white face of the Hereford, so a calf buyer knows that the sire was a specialised beef bull.

In the quest for good beef qualities, European breeds such as the Simmental from Switzerland and the Charolais and Limousin from France have been widely used for crossing with native British breeds.

Most male calves are castrated in the early weeks of life. They are then referred to as steers or bullocks. To get leaner meat some of bull beef is reared, ie the calves are not castrated, though these should be marketed before they are 15 months old.

WHAT YOU CAN DO

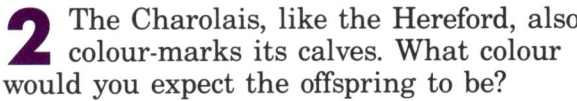

1 Why do you think the castration of bull calves helps the farmer to rear them for beef? What might be the problems of keeping bulls for beef?

2 The Charolais, like the Hereford, also colour-marks its calves. What colour would you expect the offspring to be?

3 Find out which different cuts of beef are available.

Sheep

There are almost 17 million breeding ewes on farms in the UK. Sheep are kept for both their meat and wool. Three main types of sheep are kept:

Hill and Upland Small, hardy, late-maturing breeds such as the Scottish Blackface and Swaledale, which thrive on rough hill grazing and can resist bad weather conditions with a long, hard-wearing fleece.

Lowland Earlier maturing breeds with a high quality fleece such as the Border Leicester or the Clun Forest used widely for crossing.

Downland Breeds such as the Suffolk or Dorset Down widely used with cross-bred ewes for the production of early maturing quality lamb.

Farmers in different parts of the country depend on cross-breeding to produce the ewes or lambs they want for their own particular needs and conditions.

WHAT YOU CAN DO

Look at the cross-breeding pattern illustrated below.

Breeding chart for prime lamb production

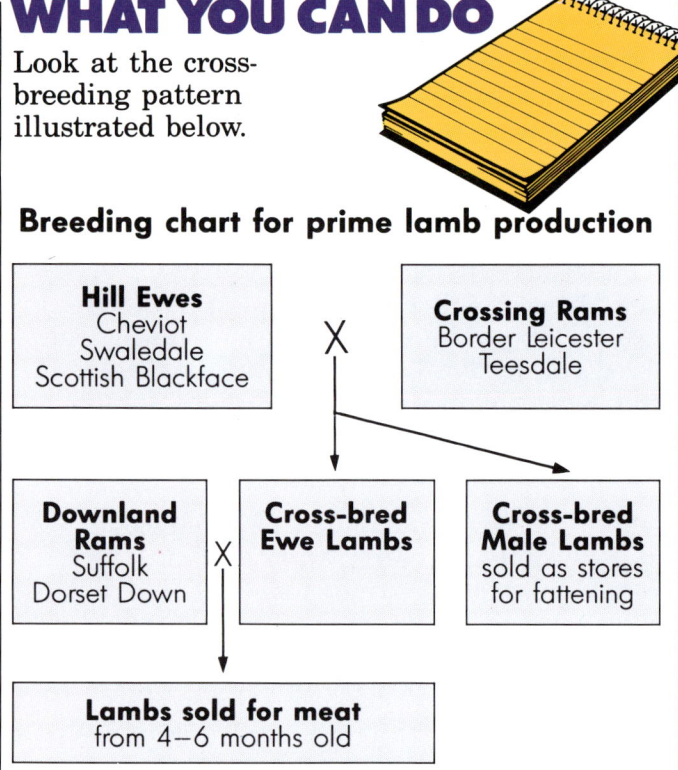

Can you work out which characteristics are passed on to the lambs in the breeding chart?

A hill sheep farm in the English Lake District

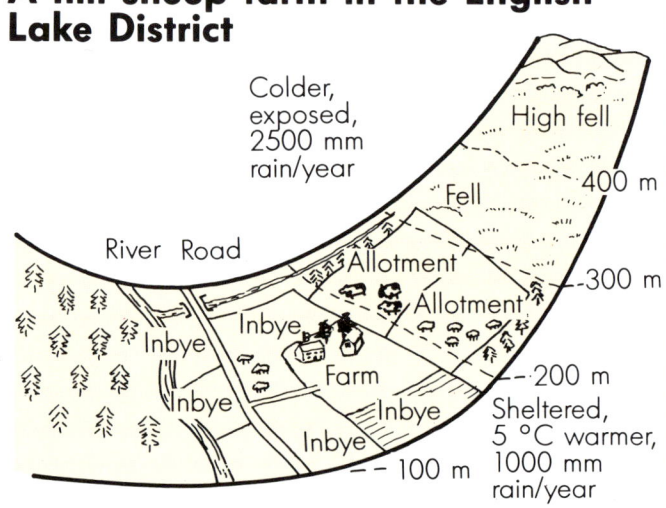

The following terms have specific meanings in the Lake District.

Fell and High Fell — unenclosed common land, rough moorland grazing

Allotment — enclosed rough grazing

Inbye — lower fields close to farm for grazing, forage crops and lambing

WHAT YOU CAN DO

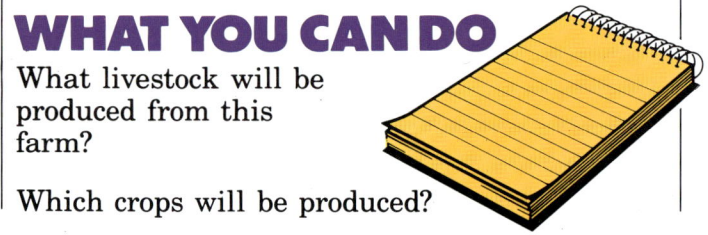

What livestock will be produced from this farm?

Which crops will be produced?

Pigs

There are about 800 000 breeding sows and eight million pigs on UK farms.

There are two main systems of keeping breeding sows:

- *intensive* (the great majority of herds today). Sows and young pigs are kept under cover in special yards or houses and grouped according to age

- *extensive*. Sows and their litters are kept out of doors foraging for part of their diet and have a simple form of shelter.

Nearly all weaned pigs kept for fattening for bacon and pork are kept indoors.

A breeding sow produces about two litters a year with 9–12 piglets in each litter. Pork pigs are usually 4–5 months old when they are marketed; bacon pigs 5–6 months old.

Breeding chart for intensive modern bacon pig production

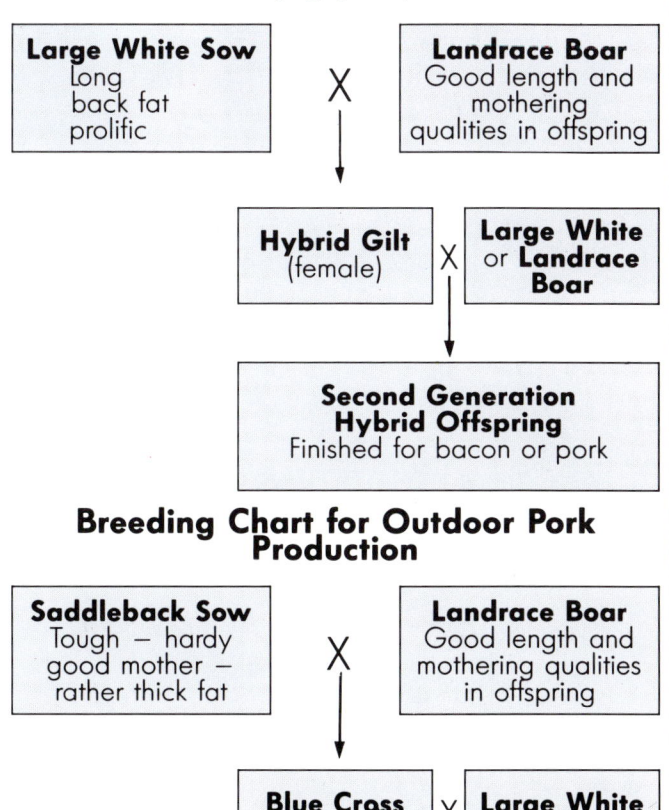

| **Large White Sow** Long back fat prolific | X | **Landrace Boar** Good length and mothering qualities in offspring |

Hybrid Gilt (female) X **Large White** or **Landrace Boar**

Second Generation Hybrid Offspring Finished for bacon or pork

Breeding Chart for Outdoor Pork Production

| **Saddleback Sow** Tough – hardy good mother – rather thick fat | X | **Landrace Boar** Good length and mothering qualities in offspring |

Blue Cross Hybrid gilt X **Large White** or **Landrace**

Finished pork pigs

Why is cross-breeding used? What advantages will the piglets inherit?

The Sow Cycle

Pregnancy lasts for 115 days. When the sow is due to farrow (indoors), she is put into a separate farrowing crate which stops her crushing her piglets. It also enables the farmer to supervise the births and check the health of the newly born piglets. The piglets have to be kept very warm so a covered 'creep' with a heat lamp is provided.

Piglets are weaned from the sow at three–five weeks old. The sow should then return to the boar within seven days so she can have two litters a year.

Pigs reared for bacon are fattened in warm conditions on concentrated cereals and protein feeds fed either dry or with water or surplus skimmed milk. Pork pigs are usually fed in the same way, but are sometimes fattened on waste foods such as boiled swill.

WHAT YOU CAN DO

1 Do you think that that farrowing crates are a good idea for (a) the sow and (b) the piglets?

2 Why do you think piglets need to be kept warm?

Poultry

We eat 12.7 billion eggs a year in the UK. They are used in all sorts of ways from the traditional English breakfast to cakes and puddings.

The term poultry includes chickens, turkeys, ducks and geese. Chickens, which are the most important in this country, are kept either for egg production (layers) or for table meat (broilers). Broilers and turkeys account for over one quarter of the whole meat market.

The modern poultry industry is based on the use of technology in which the control of diet, environment and genetics all play a part. Systems range from intensive units to barn and free-range systems. Each system needs particular management skills and together they offer the consumer a choice.

A large poultry unit might consist of as many as 100 000 birds, housed in large, low, windowless buildings in which the environment − light, heat and ventilation − is very carefully controlled. Each bird must also have a minimum amount of space. All this ensures that they keep healthy and warm.

Under the intensive battery cage system, with its mechanised feeding, cleaning, watering and collection of eggs, the production of eggs has increased enormously and their relative cost has come down. Laying birds may also be kept on deep litter in indoor houses, though costs of production are higher on this system.

Broilers (chicken for meat) grow quickly in intensive rearing houses. When they are ready to be marketed, the carcasses can be deep frozen for easy storage and distribution. We now produce nearly 500 million chickens a year. This intensive system has enabled chicken to be more widely available at low prices, and to be used in many processed foods.

WHAT YOU CAN DO

1 How do you think the environment of the birds is controlled?

2 Look at the photograph of free-range hens. What are the advantages and disadvantages of keeping poultry in this way?

The care and feeding of farm animals

Digestion is the process which makes the food that is eaten soluble and capable of absorption into the bloodstream. The blood then transports these digested food products to all parts of the body.

The digestive system breaks large food molecules down into smaller molecules, for example:

Carbohydrates   into   sugars
Fats and oils   into   fatty acids and glycerol
Proteins   into   amino-acids

Vitamins and minerals are readily absorbed into the body as they do not need to be broken down further.

Cattle and sheep have a different digestive system to pigs, poultry and humans. They have four stomach compartments while pigs and humans only have one. One of the four stomachs is very big — the rumen — and this is packed with bacteria and protozoa which break down fibrous foods such as grass and forage crops. Pigs, poultry and humans can only deal with very small amounts of fibrous foods, so their rations (or diet) must consist of concentrated foods such as cereals, proteins, legumes, vegetables or processed foods.

A Balanced Diet
For all animals, a range of foods — carbohydrates, fats and oils, proteins, vitamins, minerals and water — is essential for good health and growth. Deficiencies can lead to disease and ill health.

Hygiene and Health

It is essential for farmers to keep their animals in hygienic conditions and in good health.

What are the problems of rearing large numbers of animals intensively?

Buildings must be kept as clean and well ventilated as possible. Modern buildings are designed to be cleaned easily. Beef cattle and pigs are sometimes housed on slatted floors while concrete aisles in the cow cubicle house allow the easy passage of the dung scraper.

In the milking parlour, the strictest hygiene must be maintained if the milk that we drink is to be absolutely clean. The farmer is heavily penalised if he supplies contaminated milk to the Milk Marketing Board.

The control of parasites

Farm animals often pick up parasites which affect both their health and performance. External parasites such as lice or ticks live in the animal's coat or hair. These are killed by insecticides. Others are internal parasites, such as stomach worms or liver fluke which can be controlled by drenching or injection.

The control of animal disease

The control and eradication of disease continues to be the subject of a great deal of research. Many diseases such as diarrhoea in calves or pigs are treated directly with antibiotics or similar methods of control. Inoculation is widely used to protect animals from diseases by building up in the body an immunity against a particular organism.

Tuberculosis in cattle has been virtually eradicated in the UK since 1966, as the result

of compulsory testing and slaughter. In 1972 the Government introduced a similar scheme to eradicate Brucellosis, another serious disease causing abortion in cattle and undulant fever in humans. As a result, most dairy herds are now Brucellosis free.

Foot-and-mouth disease is the most serious disease which can break out in cattle, sheep, pigs and goats. Outbreaks are dreaded by the farmer because the only way to control the disease is to slaughter the whole herd even if only one case is found on a farm. The animals' carcasses are burned and the farm is isolated.

Why does Britain find it easier to control infectious diseases than other countries in Europe?

Animal Welfare

The intensive production of pigs and poultry has reduced the cost of producing meat and eggs, and methods and standards of hygiene have all greatly improved in the past 30 years. Intensive farming can produce healthier animals than many free-range systems. The regular removal of droppings breaks the cycle of disease caused by parasites, and the pen system enables the farmer to check individual animals regularly. Animals kept indoors are safe from predators, eg foxes, and heating and lighting, unlike the weather, can be adjusted to suit the stock. The farmer can ensure that each animal gets enough well-balanced food and water without having to fight for it.

However, some people feel that keeping animals indoors is unnatural, unhealthy and bad for the animals. Over the years, the welfare of farm animals has been seriously considered by the Government, the farmers' organisations and other interested bodies. Codes of practice drawn up by the Farm Animals Welfare Council are now recommended and are kept under constant review. But the real safeguard is that it is in the farmer's own interest to keep his stock healthy. Animals suffering from stress or cruel treatment do not give high-quality produce.

1 The issue of animal welfare in intensive systems is controversial. What do you think are the advantages and disadvantages of intensive farming for a) the animals and b) the consumer?

2 If you were a farmer how would you keep animals for food production?

The Contribution of Agriculture to the Economy

Total receipts in 1985 were £12,123 million, almost as much as the combined turnover of the British National Oil Corporation and British Coal. Agriculture made up 2% of the total GDP of Britain's economy.

The output from British farms

The pie chart shows the value of the different products sold off British farms. It should be considered alongside the pie chart showing the cost of inputs into the farm business.

Costs of the Farm Business

The pie chart shows the breakdown of the input costs into the farm business apart from interest payments.

WHAT YOU CAN DO

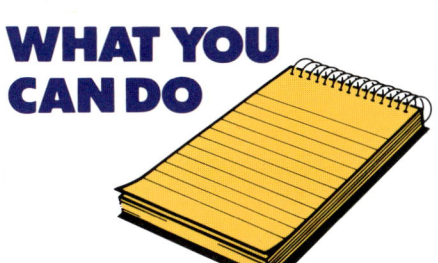

1 What are the miscellaneous costs? Give some examples.

2 What do you think is included in livestock feeds?

Value and Proportion of Total Output from British Farms 1985 (£ million)

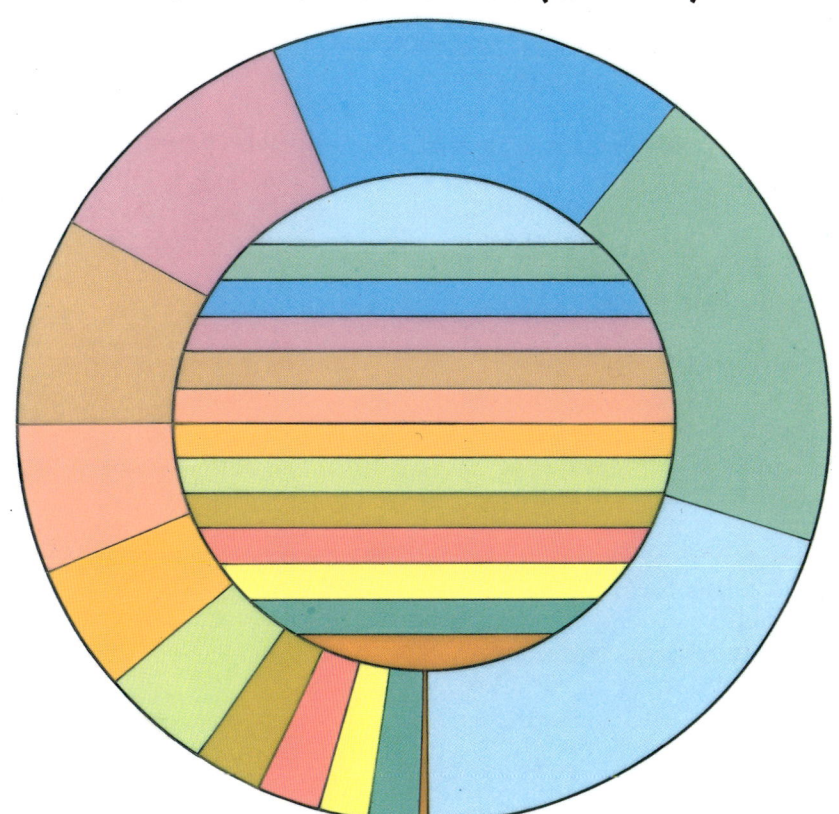

Input Costs of British Farms 1985 (£ million)

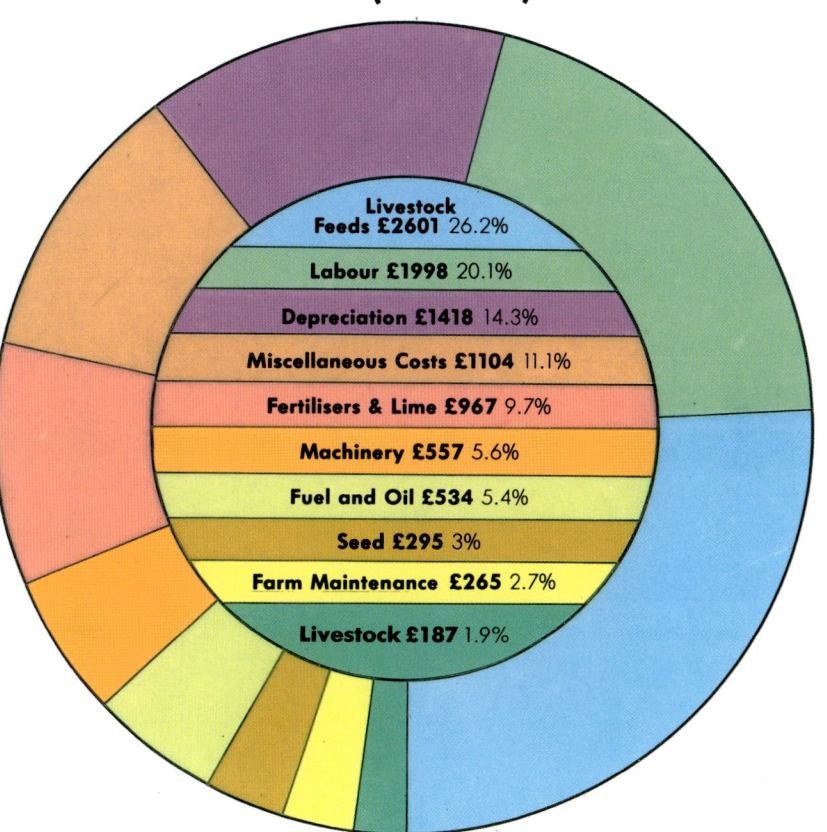

Livestock Feeds £2601 26.2%
Labour £1998 20.1%
Depreciation £1418 14.3%
Miscellaneous Costs £1104 11.1%
Fertilisers & Lime £967 9.7%
Machinery £557 5.6%
Fuel and Oil £534 5.4%
Seed £295 3%
Farm Maintenance £265 2.7%
Livestock £187 1.9%

A comparative economic study of two contrasting farms

A Welsh Hill Farm

Farm Facts

SIZE AND LAND USE: 126 ha; 74 ha hill grazing; 52 ha enclosed pasture

LIVESTOCK: 12 suckler beef cows, 400 breeding ewes, 440 lambs sold, 50 – 75 ewe lambs kept

CROPS: Grass: silage 200 t; hay 10t

WORKFORCE: 2 part-time

MACHINERY: 2 tractors; baler; sprayer; fertiliser spreader; plough

COSTS:

11 t of fertiliser and lime	£1 896
8 t sheep feed	£1 840
2 t cattle feed	£636
Fuel and electricity	£1 180
Silage making contracted to outside workers	£50 per ha
Fencing	£1.76 per metre
Rent for the farm	£25 per ha

INCOME:

Cattle (including subsidies)	£3 091
Sheep (including wool sales, premiums and allowances)	£13 551

The subsidies the farmer receives are:

Hill cow subsidy	£44.50 per cow
Suckler cow premium	£24 per cow
Hill compensatory allowance	£6.25 per ewe
Annual premium	£4.75 per ewe

An Eastern Counties Arable Farm

Farm Facts

SIZE AND LAND USE: 250 ha

LIVESTOCK: None

CROPS: Winter Wheat (150 ha); Spring Barley (30 ha); Sugar beet (30 ha); Winter barley (20 ha); Oilseed rape (10 ha)

WORKFORCE: 4 full-time: 1 part-time (the farmer)

MACHINERY AND BUILDINGS: A full range

COSTS:

Variable costs	£62 500
Labour	£25 500
Machinery and power	£49 250
Rent	£27 750
Other overheads	£14 000
Total	£179 000

INCOME:

Gross income	£232 500
Net farm income	£53 500

WHEAT:

Yield per ha	6.5 t
Income per ha	£728
Expenditure per ha	£637

BARLEY:

Yield per ha	4.7 t
Income per ha	£531
Expenditure per ha	£489

WHAT YOU CAN DO

1 Note the different scale of inputs and outputs for these two farms and compare the relative incomes and capital investment needed.

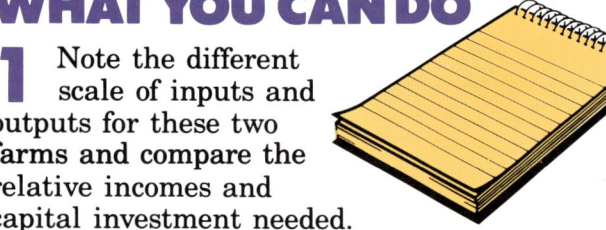

Marketing and the consumer

People's tastes and eating habits have been influenced in recent years by various factors. One is the growth in ownership of fridges and freezers. Can you list some others?

There is a demand for a greater variety of products including convenience and imported foods. More people are eating out, buying take-away foods and 'picking-their-own' fruit and vegetables.

Today two thirds of all the grocery trade is handled by the major supermarkets such as Sainsburys, Tesco, Co-op and ASDA. This has provided the consumer with a wide range of produce at very competitive prices. It has also put pressure on farmers and growers to supply produce of high quality in specific quantities at certain times of the year or on a continuing basis.

Traditionally, Britain has been an importer rather than an exporter of food. But greater efforts are now being made to export products such as cereals, meat and speciality foods such as Stilton cheese.

WHAT YOU CAN DO

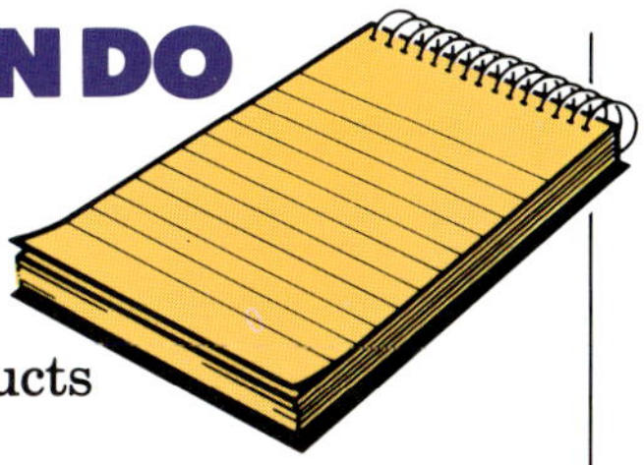

1 Find out the names of the organisations that promote:

    Milk and dairy products
    Potatoes
    Wool
    Apples and pears
    Meat

2 What else do they do?

Organic Farming

Over the last few years there has been an increasing demand for organic produce – food that is grown without the use of artificial fertilisers or pesticides. Why do you think this is?

Organic foods tend to be produced by small-scale farms. There are probably about 1000 organic farmers in Britain, mainly in Wales and the South West of England. Organic produce usually needs more labour, and is therefore more expensive to grow, and yields are often lower than under conventional systems. However, other costs of production may be lower. Some people will pay up to 33% more for certain types of organically produced food.

WHAT YOU CAN DO

1 In what ways is organic farming different from general farming practice?

2 Why are organic farms more labour intensive?

3 What are the benefits and what are the costs?

4 (a) How large do you think the demand is?
(b) Do you think organic farming has a future in Britain?

Farming and the countryside

Many features of our present landscape were created by landowners and farmers in previous generations. We are now feeling the impact of a technological revolution. The actions of farmers over the past 40 years, and the changes they will make in the years ahead, will determine the countryside of tomorrow.

What farmers are doing to protect the countryside

We cannot go back to the past and we must all eat. Farmers, like everybody else, have responded to the new technologies. Consumers demand a ready supply of high-quality foods throughout the year. At the same time, the natural resources of the countryside must be conserved. How can we resolve this?

Farmers are becoming increasingly aware of the importance of conservation and of ways in which the needs both of modern farming and conservation can be combined successfully on their farms. There are now many interesting and effective initiatives all over the country.

● **Trees**   In the last five years, 29 million trees have been planted on some 46 000 farms. This has more than replaced the 20 million elm trees killed by Dutch elm disease.

● **Ponds**   There are over 170 000 ponds in England and Wales. Although 10 000 were filled in in the last five years, 22 000 new ponds have been created.

● **Hedgerows**   There are now an estimated 500 000 kilometres of hedges. Up until the mid-1970s, many hedgerows were removed mainly in arable areas in order to create larger fields. Although there has been considerable replanting, hedges are still being lost at a faster rate than they are being replaced.

Most farms have pockets of land which are either an awkward shape or size. Many farmers are realising that such areas can be developed into natural habitats and that the wildlife they attract can help the farmer. Insect-eating birds can help to reduce damage to crops. Nest boxes for bats and owls which eat insects and mice, are cheap and easy to install.

Most farmers and their staff live where they work so it is in their own interest to maintain a pleasant and attractive environment. But responsibility goes much farther than this and many landowners and farmers are aware that they hold the land in trust for future generations.

A 1930s farm

Smaller fields	Older type machines at
More hedges	work, eg binder,
Ponds	perhaps horses
Farmyard and traditional	
buildings	
Elm trees	

B 1980s farm

Larger fields	Slurry lagoon
Fewer hedges and trees	Grain silo
New copses for wildlife	Large machines at work,
New ponds	eg combine harvester
Groupings of new	
purpose-built buildings	
(with screening by	
trees)	

WHAT YOU CAN DO

1 Would farm A support a greater variety of wildlife?

2 List four habitats on each farm and name the wildlife you think would occupy them.

3 A local conservation task force offers Farmer B free labour. He agrees to contribute £500 to improving habitats on the farm. How do you think he might use both the labour and the money to best advantage?

Try to draw up a list of jobs and materials he might need and could afford. Then draw up your plan of action.

4 Why did farmers need to enlarge their fields? What effect did this have?

How much do you think it costs to create a new pond or to plant a small area in trees? Is the farmer likely to get a return on his outlay (a) in the short term or (b) in the long term?

Look at the three diagrams showing the changing use of a piece of farm land over the last 50 years and the number of breeding birds that it supports.

You can see that more food can be produced as more land is available on which to grow crops. What effect does the changing land use have on the variety of bird life?

How important do you think this is?

Do you think new laws are needed to deal with any of the problems in the countryside? What do you know about existing laws and the way in which they work? Is the legal approach the best way to deal with countryside issues?

The changing use of farmland and bird populations if an arable system is carried to extremes

1 Blue tit
2 Whitethroat
3 Great tit
4 Songthrush
5 Crow
6 Long tailed tit
7 Kestrel
8 Greenfinch
9 Moorhen
10 Reed bunting
11 Sedge warbler
12 Partridge
13 Pheasant
14 Lapwing
15 Skylark
16 Dunnock
17 Wren
18 Blackbird
19 Corn bunting
20 Yellowhammer
21 Chaffinch
22 Robin

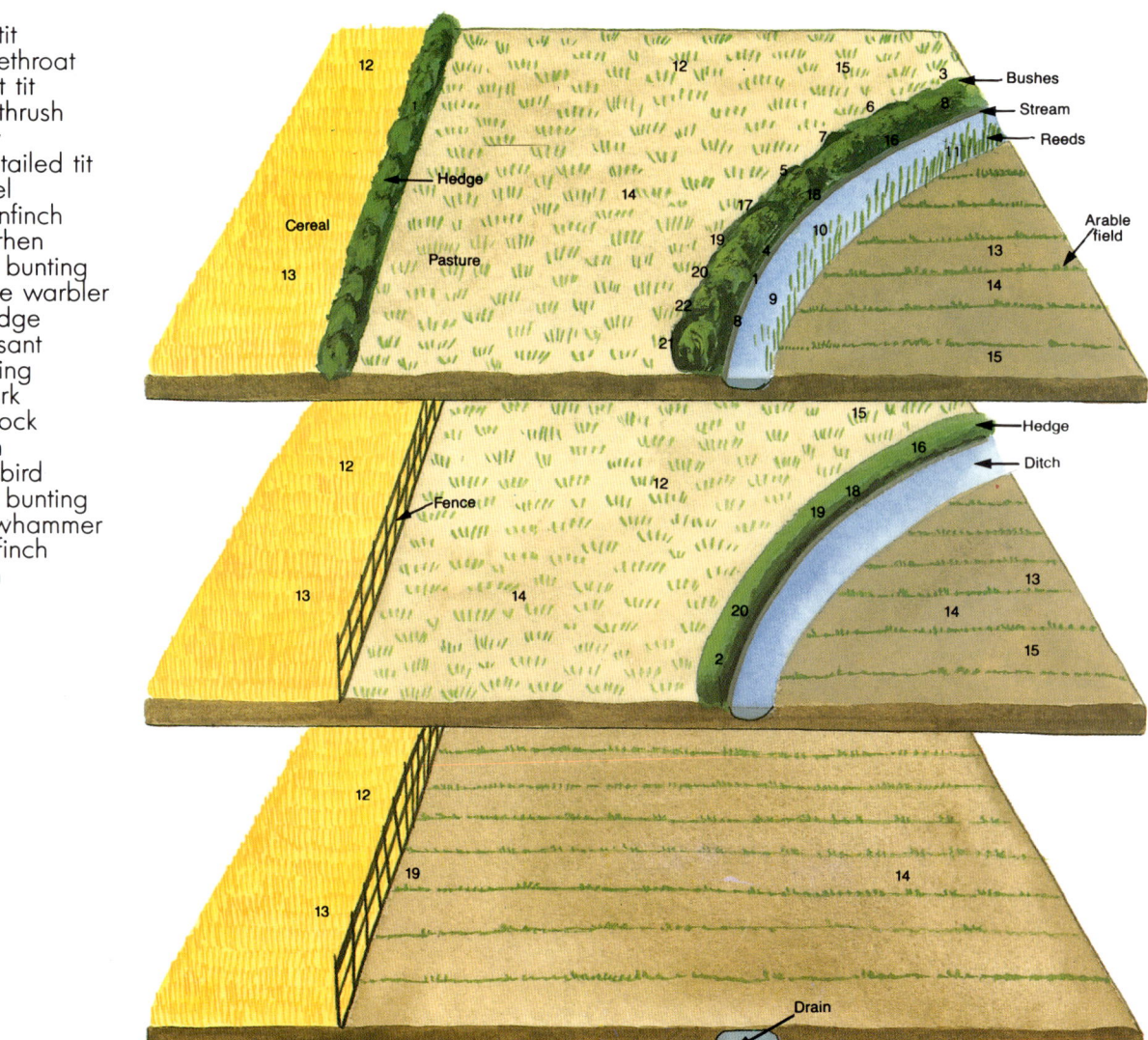

Some controversial issues

As modern farming relies more on the use of fertilisers and pesticides and other new techniques, some issues have arisen that cause concern to farmers and conservationists alike.

The use of Nitrogen Fertilisers. Most farm soils contain large quantities of organic nitrogen, but this is only available to plants in small amounts. If crops are to reach their full potential and give an economic return, nitrogen fertilisers must be added. But the soil activity caused by boosting the nitrate means that sometimes nitrate may leach (percolate) into drainage water.

The use of Pesticides. Pesticides must be applied in the right amounts and in the recommended way. The goal of scientists is to identify naturally occurring chemicals which are only toxic to the target pest and they are continually working on equipment to apply pesticides more accurately.

The Disposal of Waste. Large numbers of animals kept together in intensive conditions create slurry (liquid manure). On most farms slurry is either held in 'lagoons' or in underground storage tanks until it is pumped out and spread on the land. Farmers must prevent slurry (and the effluent from silage) from seeping out and polluting waterways and killing fish.

Straw Burning. For many arable farmers, burning is the only way to get rid of waste cereal straw for which there is no market.

Waste straw lying in fields can become a major fire hazard. A well-controlled, planned burn removes straw rapidly and completely, kills weed seeds and speeds up cultivations for the next crop. Farmers have developed their own straw and stubble burning code which is backed by bylaws. Meanwhile, scientists are searching for ways to use the surplus straw crop, and farmers are working with scientists to find ways of successfully incorporating the straw into the soil.

Access and Recreation. People who live in towns enjoy escaping into the countryside at weekends and on holiday. Farmers, quite understandably, get annoyed if visitors to what is, in effect, their workplace are thoughtless in their behaviour.

WHAT YOU CAN DO

1 What do you think the alternatives to straw burning might be? What problems might be experienced by a farmer wishing to work the straw and stubble back into the soil?

2 What might ramblers do that would upset farmers and what do farmers do that might annoy ramblers? How can both groups be satisfied?

3 To some extent we are all responsible for pollution of our environment. Can you suggest ways in which we do this?

Conservation Organisations and Groups

A range of official and voluntary organisations exist to protect and conserve the countryside. People from all walks of life are involved.

The two principal statutory (Government funded) bodies are the Countryside Commission and the Nature Conservancy Council. The NCC is responsible for Sites of Special Scientific Interest (SSSIs) and Nature Reserves.

WHAT YOU CAN DO

. . . about derelict land, dirty ponds and streams, broken walls or lack of habitats. There is much that all of us can do either by giving money or through actual work.

Two bodies which aim to attract young people who want to become more deeply involved in farming and the countryside are the National Trust for Conservation Volunteers and Young Farmers' Clubs. You do not have to be a farmer to join a YFC.

Find out what the letters RSPB and FWAG stand for, and what the organisations do. Do you think that groups like these have an important part to play in looking after our wildlife and countryside?

How does the Government help?
Landowners and farmers often find it difficult on economic grounds to justify the planting of trees or devoting land to conservation. Why? This difficulty has been recognised by the Government, and in certain cases, financial help is available.

WHAT YOU CAN DO

1 How long does it take for a broad-leaved tree such as a lime to reach maturity?

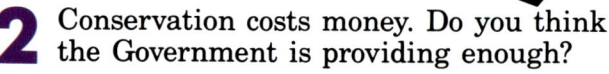

2 Conservation costs money. Do you think the Government is providing enough?

3 If people want a certain sort of countryside, who should pay?

7 Starvation and surpluses

The Overcrowded Planet

The United Nations predicts that the population of the world will reach 6000 million by the year 2000.

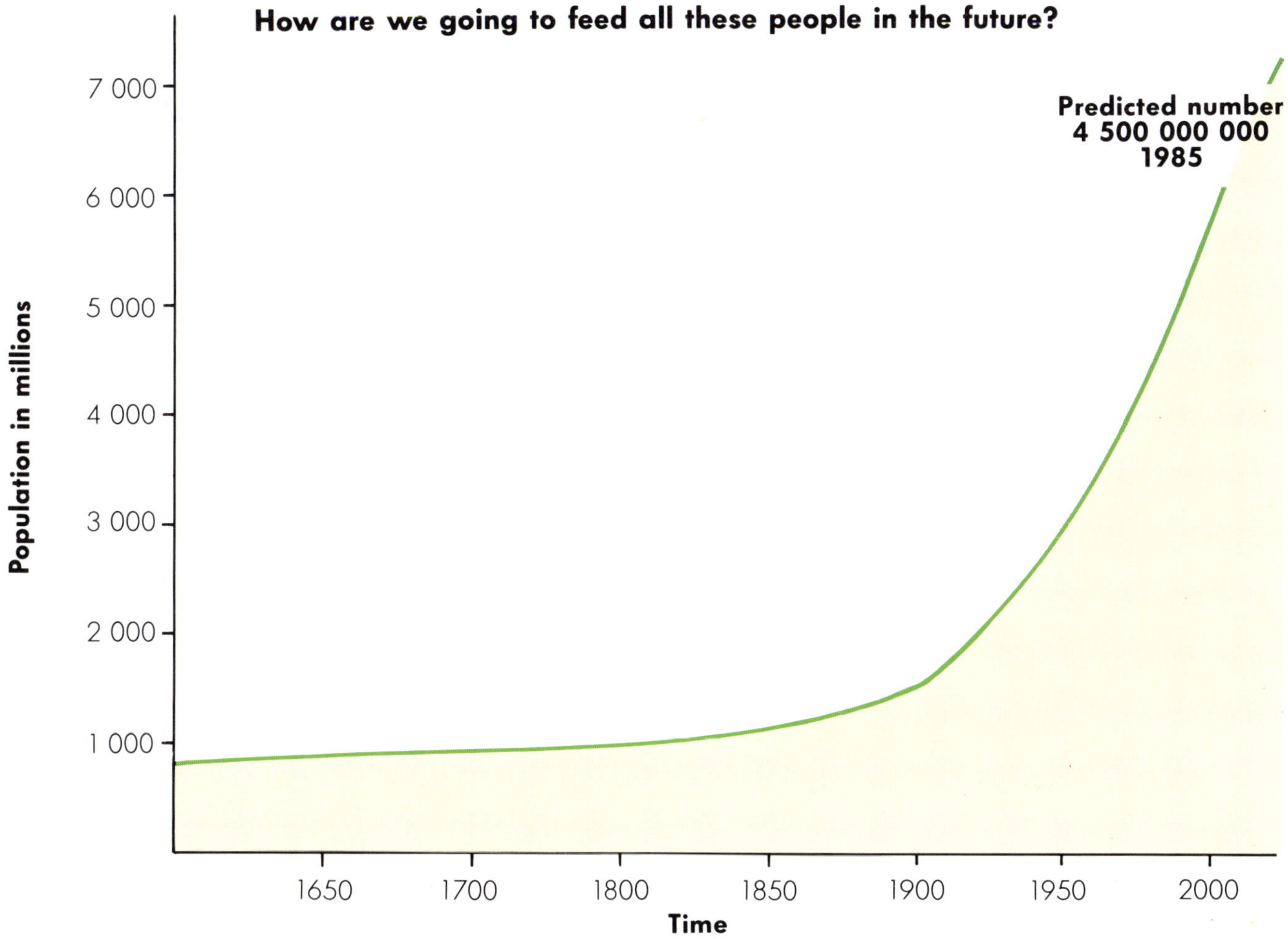

How are we going to feed all these people in the future?

**Predicted number
4 500 000 000
1985**

Population in millions (y-axis): 1 000, 2 000, 3 000, 4 000, 5 000, 6 000, 7 000

Time (x-axis): 1650, 1700, 1800, 1850, 1900, 1950, 2000

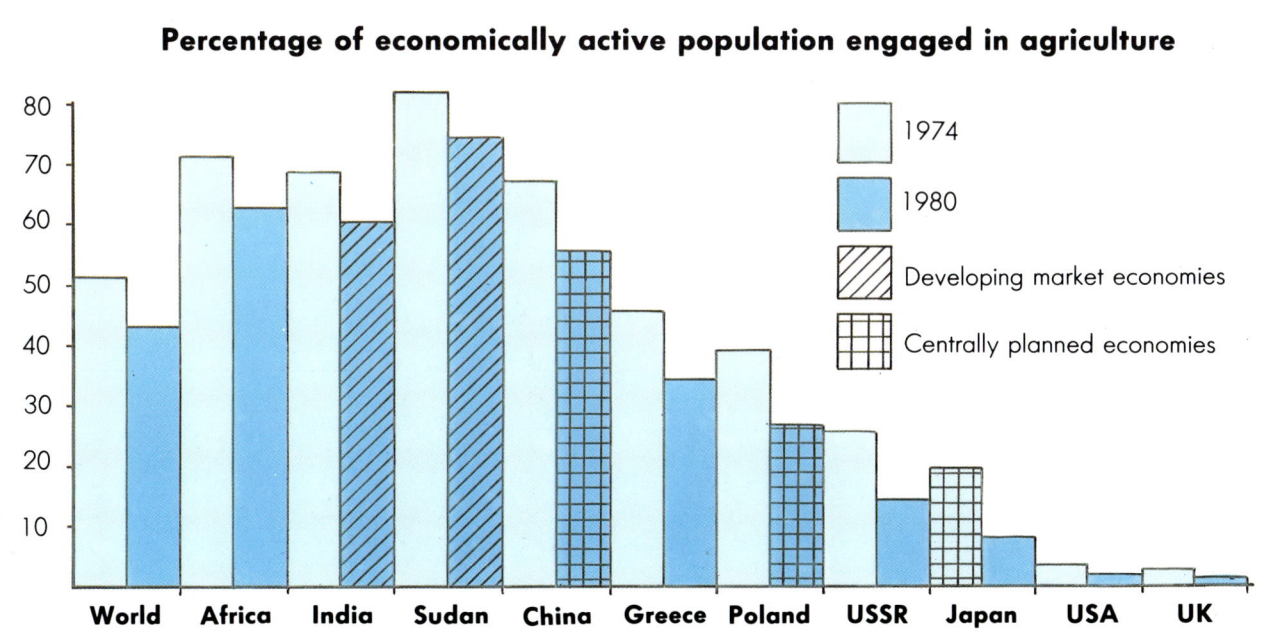

Percentage of economically active population engaged in agriculture

Legend:
- 1974
- 1980
- Developing market economies
- Centrally planned economies

Categories: World, Africa, India, Sudan, China, Greece, Poland, USSR, Japan, USA, UK

Agriculture in Third World countries

Agriculture in many Third World countries is barely above the subsistence level and 500 million people are still hungry.

The reasons for this are complex and varied. Unfavourable climates, poor-quality soils, lack of expertise and finance to exploit technological developments all limit agricultural production, and high birth-rates mean that more food is needed.

Equally important is Government policy. Sympathetic Government policies aimed at keeping the rural population on the land and helping them to produce more food can overcome many problems of geography and climate. Government policies in India and China have helped farmers achieve spectacular advances in food production in recent years.

WHAT YOU CAN DO

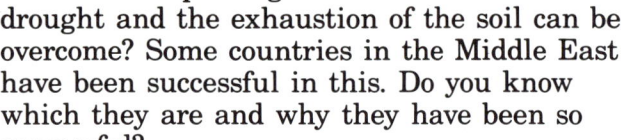

How do you think countries in the Third World could produce more of their own food? Are there ways in which the effects of prolonged drought and the exhaustion of the soil can be overcome? Some countries in the Middle East have been successful in this. Do you know which they are and why they have been so successful?

How do surpluses occur?

It is only in relatively recent times that surpluses have occurred regularly in countries with modern farming systems. Before that, food shortages were frequent. Why do you think this change has come about?

Why is the Common Agricultural Policy (CAP) now producing so many surpluses?

Every year the Council of Ministers of the EC meets to set the support levels for that year's farm prices. For some major products they also set intervention prices, that is, the prices at which surpluses will be taken off the market.

If prices fall to this lower level, Government agencies intervene to buy up the produce to prevent any further fall in the price. The products are then put into stores. These form the famous grain and butter 'mountains' and olive oil and wine 'lakes'. Many farm products, for example, pigs, poultry and most fruit and vegetables, do not get such support.

The problem lies in the fact that the EC has often tended to set prices at a level which encourages further production with no restrictions imposed on how much farmers can produce. Recently, quotas on production have been introduced for some commodities. Find out what they are.

Most members of the EC, including Britain, accept that changes are needed in the CAP to reduce its costs and surplus production. However, it is very difficult to get 12 very different countries with different political and farming traditions to agree on how the CAP should be reformed. Why do you think this is?

One way of reforming the CAP is to encourage farmers to grow crops not in surplus. For example, the UK imports over 90% of the timber it uses. But farmland planted with trees produces no income for at least 25 years. A way needs to be found to help farmers during the critical period between planting the trees and receiving income from thinnings and felling. What costs will the farmer have to meet? In what other ways could the CAP be reformed?

Could food aid prevent starvation?
Short term = food needed quickly

When crises like the one in 1985 in Ethiopia and the Sudan occur it is essential in the short term to send food aid at once to try to stop people dying from starvation. Try to find out the causes of the crisis in Ethiopia and Sudan.

In situations like this, grain is the easiest commodity to handle and it is used as a basic food by most people. Getting grain to the people who need it most can be very difficult. Why is this?

Long term = planning and planting

Try to find out how development aid aims to help people in the Third World.

WHAT YOU CAN DO

1 How do you think surpluses are stored in good condition?

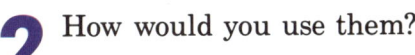

2 How would you use them?

3 Which products would not be helpful to a country like Ethiopia?

All these ideas are already being practised in some parts of the world, but some are likely to develop more than others in the years to come.

Mass Fermentation Mass fermentation of carbohydrates from straw and animal wastes or from cereals and potatoes produces alcohol for fuel.

Industrial Genetics Genetic engineers can transfer genes from one organism to another. This is now being carried out in bacteria and fungi. Research is proceeding into transferring genes which permit bacterial fixation of nitrogen in legume roots into other plants such as cereals.

Protein Bacteria can be used to work on liquid farm wastes and convert them to suitable animal feed protein.

Environmental Technology Artificial environments can be created to grow crops in otherwise unsuitable areas.

Plant Breeding Crops such as Canadian wheats have been bred to mature in a short growing season to suit special climatic conditions, and could lead to two crops being grown each year.

Protein from Plants Protein derived from plants like soya beans is not attractive to eat, but advances in food texturing are making it better. In that case, animals, which convert plant food into meat, would become less essential.

Sea Farming There is a potential of 120 million tonnes of protein and oil from fish. At the moment less than half of this is being fished. This proportion could be increased if the oceans were properly 'managed'.

Fish Farming Fish farms have been established in estuary basins as well as in freshwater lakes and streams.

Biomass The term biomass describes a total production of organic matter regardless of its composition.

Organic matter can then be used either as fuel or for mass fermentation to produce methane gas.

Controlled Hothouse Production Large environmentally controlled hothouses could produce crops continuously using water culture (hydroponics) as the growing medium rather than soil.

WHAT YOU CAN DO

Choose one of these topics and try to find out more about it. What are the problems at the moment? What advantages could this system have in the future?

Glossary

Annual premium — sum of money paid for a commodity annually, such as a grant to a farmer

Aphid — insect pest of plants, greenfly being one of the commonest

Aspect (of land) — the way in which land slopes, especially whether towards or away from the sun

Baler — machine for compressing hay, straw or other commodities into tight bundles

Beef suckler cows — cows kept to produce calves suitable for beef production, the cow suckling the calves for 5-6 months

Bin tipper — a machine which gently tips bins of produce, especially fruit, into a store or into a hopper for a grading line

Biomass — as defined on page 44

Bread wheat — wheat has to have a high gluten content for breadmaking, so that the air bubbles made by the yeast are trapped and the bread rises well. In the UK it produces lower yields than wheat which is only suitable for animal feed

Broiler — a chicken raised for meat production

Celery grader — machine for grading celery by size

Combine drill — machine which sows seeds and applies fertiliser to the seed bed at the same time

Conservation — in its literal sense, means keeping something safely: hay and silage are conserved grass. Conservation of the countryside means keeping it safely, but not in the sense of preserving it totally unchanged as in a museum

Corn drill — machine for sowing seeds

Corn dryer — machine used to blow warm air through grain to reduce the moisture content and prevent the grain becoming mouldy

Creep — heated area where piglets go for warmth and food away from the sow

Cross breeding — mating two different breeds together. This is usually done to combine some of the best qualities of each parent in the offspring

Dairy grass — grass grown for dairy cattle or silage

Deep litter — an indoor system for raising poultry where the floor is covered with litter and the hens can scratch around

Disc harrow — a machine which cuts and consolidates the soil; it can also be used to cut up stubble and crop residues

Drenching — giving medicine to an animal by pouring a drench down its throat

Dutch barn — a high barn with open sides for storing hay or straw

Establishment (of a crop) — period when a crop is starting to grow

Farrowing crate — a series of protective metal rails around the sow which allow the piglets to escape from her during the first few days to avoid the danger of being crushed by her

Feed block — concentrated food for animals, which they can lick, processed into blocks

Finishing — the last stages of growing a crop or fattening up animals

Forage crops — leafy food for animals

Forage harvester — a machine used to cut different types of green material mainly for silage making

Furrow slice — the slice of soil cut and turned over when ploughing

Habitat — the natural environment of a plant or animal

Harrow (verb) — to break up lumps of soil to make a fine seed bed

Hectare — a metric quantity of land equivalent to 2.47 acres (there are 100 to 1km²)

Heifer followers — female calves being reared to replace older cows in the herd

Herbicide — chemical compound to kill weeds

Hill cow subsidy — payment made to farmers who breed beef cattle in upland areas

Hybrid — the product of two or more pure lines (plants or animals) which produce a superior plant or animal

Lactation — the period a cow is in milk, approximately 305 days, following birth of a calf

Legumes — plants with bacterial nodules in their roots which produce seeds in pods — beans, peas

Ley — temporary grass, especially grass meant to be ploughed up again one year, or a few years, after sowing

Loam — a rich soil consisting mainly of sand and clay, a balanced mixture of light and heavy soil

Malt — extract from sprouted grain which is used for making beer, whisky and other foodstuffs

Mangold — also called mangel — is a crop grown for feeding to livestock on the farm

Milking parlours — a small specially equipped building where cows are milked in rotation in a limited number of stalls

Oilseed rape — a crop which is grown for its seed which is rich in oil. The oil can be used to make cooking oil, margarine, paints, chemicals, etc.

Permanent grass — better quality grassland which is not normally ploughed (see rough grazing)

Pests — all organisms which are harmful to us either directly or by affecting the food that we eat

Polisher — machine used to polish the fruit before it is packed

Potash — one of the main plant foods needed to keep plants healthy and to improve quality

Protozoa — minute single-cell organisms, some of which, like bacteria, help to break down food

Rotary cultivator — a machine with rotating blades used to break up the soil

Rotation — a system of farming by which different crops are grown on the same land in a carefully planned sequence

Rough grazing — poorer-quality grassland, often not capable of being ploughed or reseeded

Ruminants — animals, including cattle, sheep, goats and deer which have a divided stomach specially designed to deal with the fibre in grass and which chew the cud

Selective breeding — choosing individual plants or animals for reproduction because of their special characteristics

Sepal — one of the divisions of the whorl of leaves forming the outer covering of the flower bud

Silage — the product of green crops preserved for winter use by a pickling and compression process

Silo — storage building for grain or silage, a tower silo (vertical storage), or clamp silo (horizontal storage)

Silt — a fine soil originally carried by running water and deposited as sediment

Slurry — semi-liquid animal waste, stored and then spread on fields as a fertiliser

Soil fertility — the capacity of the soil to produce crops, dependent on its nutrient supply

Speciality foods — unusual foods for which there is a demand in a particular type of market

Strain — a type within a variety of animal or plant

Subsoil — a layer of material lying below the true topsoil

Suckler cow premium — money paid to a farmer for a beef cow suckling its calf

Sward — expanse of grass, a term usually used when grass is grazed

Swill — kitchen waste fed to pigs after being boiled

Threshing — separating the grain from the corn, usually done by a combine harvester

Top dress — to spread fertiliser over a growing crop

Vining peas — field peas grown for cutting with a mechanical harvester

Weaner pigs — young pigs which are gradually changing their diet from mother's milk to solid food

Winter and spring cereals — cereals which are planted in the autumn and spring, respectively

Yield — the total amount of crop produced from an area of land or of milk or meat from an animal

Sources of further information (please send an A4 sae)

Apple and Pear Development Council
Union House
The Pantiles
Tunbridge Wells
Kent

Association of Agriculture
Victoria Chambers
16–20 Strutton Ground
London SW1P 2HP

Provides advice and information under the following headings: *British Agriculture, Cereals and Other Crops, The Environment and Technology, Dairy Farming and Milk Production, Livestock and Meat, The History of Farming*, and *Horticulture*, and will supply fuller information on the case study farms.

British Agrochemicals Association
4 Lincoln Court
Lincoln Road
Peterborough PE1 2RP

British Egg Information Council
Agriculture House
Knightsbridge
London SW1X 7NJ

British Farm Produce Council
417–418 Market Towers
New Covent Garden Market
1 Nine Elms Lane
London SW8 5NQ

British Sugar Bureau
140 Park Lane
London W1Y 3AA

British Wool Marketing Board
Education Department
Oak Mills
Station Road
Clayton
Bradford
West Yorkshire

Butter Information Council
Tubs Hill House
London Road
Sevenoaks
Kent TN13 1BL

Careers Education & Training Advice Centre
National Agricultural Centre
Stoneleigh
Kenilworth
Warwickshire CV8 2LZ

Commission of the European Communities
8 Storey's Gate
London SW1P 3AT

Countryside Commission for England and Wales
John Dower House
Crescent Place
Cheltenham
Gloucestershire GL50 3RA

Countryside Commission for Scotland
Battleby
Redgorton
Perth PH1 3EW

Farming and Wildlife Advisory Group
The Lodge
Sandy
Bedfordshire SG19 2DL

Fertiliser Manufacturers' Association
Greenhill House
90–93 Cowcross Street
London EC1M 6BH

Flour Advisory Bureau
21 Arlington Street
London SW1A 1RN

Food from Britain
301-344 Market Towers
New Covent Garden Market
London SW8 5NQ

Forestry Commission
231 Corstophine Road
Edinburgh
EH12 7AT

Fresh Fruit & Vegetable Information Bureau
Bury House
126-128 Cromwell Road
London SW7 4ET

Health and Safety Executive
Room 014
St Hugh's House
Stanley Precinct
Bootle
Merseyside L20 3QY

Meat and Livestock Commission
PO Box 44
Queensway House
Bletchley
Milton Keynes
MK2 2EF

Milk Marketing Board
Thames Ditton
Surrey K17 0EL

Ministry of Agriculture, Fisheries and Food
(Publications)
Lion House
Willowburn Trading Estate
Alnwick
Northumberland

Museum of English Rural Life (and Institute of Agricultural History)
University of Reading
Whiteknights
Reading
Berkshire RG6 2AG

National Dairy Council
National Dairy Centre
Education Department
6 John Princes Street
London W1M 0AP

National Farmers' Union
Farming Information Centre
Agricultural House
Knightsbridge
London SW1X 7NJ

National Farmers' Union of Scotland
17 Grosvenor Crescent
Edinburgh EH12 5EN

Nature Conservancy Council
Publications Department
Northminster House
Peterborough PE1 1UA

Potato Marketing Board
50 Hans Crescent
London SW1X 0NB

The Royal Society for the Protection of Birds
The Lodge
Sandy
Bedfordshire
SG19 2DL

Index

PRINTED IN BELGIUM BY

INTERNATIONAL BOOK PRODUCTION